Going to Water.

American Big-Game Hunting
The Book of the Boone and Crockett Club

EDITORS
THEODORE ROOSEVELT
GEORGE BIRD GRINNELL

1901

Contents

The Boone and Crockett Club
The Editors.

A Buffalo Story
George S. Anderson.

The White Goat and his Country
Owen Wister.

A Day with the Elk
Winthrop Chanler.

Old Times in the Black Hills
Roger D. Williams.

Big Game in the Rockies
Archibald Rogers.

Coursing the Prongbuck
Theodore Roosevelt.

After Wapiti in Wyoming
F. C. Crocker.

In Buffalo Days
George Bird Grinnell.

Nights with the Grizzlies
[W. D. Pickett.

The Yellowstone Park as a Game Reservation
Arnold Hague.

A Mountain Fraud
Dean Sage.

Blacktails in the Bad Lands
Bronson Rumsey.

Photographing Wild Game
W. B. Devereux.

Literature of American Big-Game Hunting

Our Forest Reservations

The Club Exhibit at the World's Fair

Constitution and By-Laws of the Club

List of Members

The sketches entitled Big Game in the Rockies, and In Buffalo Days, have already appeared in Scribner's Magazine, and are here reprinted by kind permission of Charles Scribner's Sons. Nights with the Grizzlies has appeared in the Forest and Stream, and is reprinted by permission of the Forest and Stream Publishing Co.

List of Illustrations

Going to Water
From Scribner's Magazine.

The Master of the Herd
From Scribner's Magazine.

On the Slide Rock
Photographed from nature in the Chief Mountain country, Montana, by William H. Seward, Jr.
From the Forest and Stream.

On the Heights
From Scribner's Magazine.

Stalking the Stalker
From Scribner's Magazine.

Studying the Strangers
From Scribner's Magazine.

Crossing a Drift
From Scribner's Magazine.

Two Pairs
From Scribner's Magazine.

At Mid-day
From Scribner's Magazine.

Blackfoot Indian Piskun
From Scribner's Magazine.

Through the Mist
From Scribner's Magazine.

Prospecting for Grub
From Scribner's Magazine.

The Buffalo of the Timber
Photographed from life in the Yellowstone

National Park by John Fossam. From the Forest and Stream.

A Mountain Pasture
Photographed from life in the Yellowstone National Park by W. H. Weed.

Buffalo Cows and Calves
Photographed from life in the Yellowstone National Park by John Fossam. From the Forest and Stream.

Resting
Photographed from life by T. G. Ingersoll. From the Forest and Stream.

The illustrations from Scribner's Magazine are reproduced by kind permission of Charles Scribner's Sons; those from the Forest and Stream by permission of the Forest and Stream Publishing Company.

The Boone and Crockett Club

The aims of The Boone and Crockett Club are sufficiently set forth in Article II of its Constitution, which reads as follows:

The objects of the Club shall be:

1. To promote manly sport with the rifle.

2. To promote travel and exploration in the wild and unknown, or but partially known, portions of the country.

3. To work for the preservation of the large game of this country, and, so far as possible, to further legislation for that purpose, and to assist in enforcing the existing laws.

4. To promote inquiry into and to record observations on the habits and natural history of the various wild animals.

5. To bring about among the members the interchange of opinions and ideas on hunting, travel, exploration, on the various kinds of hunting-rifles, on the haunts of game animals, etc.

The Club is organized primarily to promote manly sport with the rifle among the large game of the wilderness, to encourage travel and exploration in little-known regions of our country, and to work for game and forest preservation by the State. Attention has been paid to all three points by the Club, but especially to sport and protection. Nevertheless exploration has not been neglected. In a trip after wilderness game the hunter is perforce obliged to traverse and explore little-known regions, at least when he is in search of the rarer animals, or is desirous of reaching the best hunting-grounds; and in addition to such exploration, which is merely incidental to the ordinary hunting trip, members of the Club have done not a little original exploration for its own sake, including surveying, and geographical and geological map-making. The results of these explorations, when sufficiently noteworthy, have appeared in periodicals devoted to such subjects, or in Government reports. The present volume is devoted to big-game hunting and to questions of game preservation.

In behalf of game protection the Club works through the State for the procuring and setting apart of reservations where forests and game alike shall be protected at all seasons by the law. These great forest reservations thus become the nurseries and breeding-grounds of game and of the large wild animals which are elsewhere inevitably exterminated by the march of settlement. Already several such reservations have been established in different States, both by National and by State action—for instance, the Adirondack Reserve in New York, the Colorado Cañon Reserve in Arizona, the big timber reserves in Colorado and Washington, the island set apart in Alaska as an undisturbed breeding-ground for salmon and sea-fowl, the Yosemite Valley and the Sequoia Parks in California. The most important reservation, however, is the Yellowstone Park, which is owned by the National Government, and is the last refuge of the buffalo in this country, besides being the chief home of the elk and of many other wild beasts. This is the most striking and typical of all these reserves, and has been thought well worth special description in the present volume, with reference to its effects upon the preservation of game.

The enactment of laws prohibiting the killing of game anywhere, save at certain seasons and under certain conditions, must be left largely to the States themselves; and among the States there is the widest possible difference both as to the laws and as to the way they are enforced. It is enforcement which needs most attention. Very many of the States have good game laws, but in very few are they rigidly enforced. Maine offers a striking instance of how well they work when properly framed and administered with honesty and efficiency. There are undoubtedly many more moose, caribou, and deer in Maine now than there were twenty-five years ago; and if the Maine Legislature will see that the good work is continued, these noble beasts of the chase will continue to increase, to the delight, not only of the hunter, but of every lover of nature and of the hardy life of the wilderness, and to the very great pecuniary profit of the people of the State. In other States—Colorado, for instance—good has come from the enactment and enforcement of game laws; but in no other State have the governmental authorities acted with the wisdom displayed by those of Maine, and in no other State have the results been so noteworthy. It is greatly to be wished that such States as Washington, Idaho, Montana, and Wyoming, which inclose the best hunting-grounds now existing in the United States, would follow Maine's lead.

Another means by which the Club hopes to bring about a proper spirit for the preservation of our big game is by frowning on and discouraging among sportsmen themselves all unsportsmanlike proceedings and all needless slaughter. The Club has persistently discouraged anything tending to glorify the making of big bags of game, and it strives to discourage the killing of the females of any game species save under rigid limitations. No harm comes to any species from the destruction of a moderate number of bulls, bucks, or rams, and these are the legitimate objects for the hunter's skill. Only legitimate methods of sport should be followed; torch hunting and the slaughter of game in deep snow or in the water are held to be unsportsmanlike.

Hunting big game in the wilderness is, above all things, a sport for a vigorous and masterful people. The rifle-bearing hunter, whether he goes on foot or on horseback, whether he voyages in a canoe or travels with a dog-sled, must be sound of body and firm of mind, and must possess energy, resolution, manliness, self-reliance, and capacity for hardy self-help. In short, the big-game hunter must possess qualities without which no race can do its life-work well; and these are the very qualities which it is the purpose of this Club, so far as may be, to develop and foster.

THEODORE ROOSEVELT.
GEORGE BIRD GRINNELL.

American Big-Game Hunting

The Master of the Herd.
Photographed from life. From Forest and Stream.

A Buffalo Story

On the last day of September, 1871, I joined my regiment, then in camp near Fort Hays, Kansas. At that time the different troops of the regiment had not been assigned to their winter quarters. My own was on its way north from Texas, where it had been stationed since the close of the war. I was extremely anxious to learn what its destination was, for I had never killed any of the large game of the country; in fact, had never fired a rifle except at a target. Should my troop be ordered to Fort Riley, or Fort Harker, east of Fort Hays, or to Fort Dodge, south of Hays, I feared that my chance of meeting with large game would be doubtful. To my great delight, however, I found that my assignment was to Fort Lyon, situated on the northern bank of the Arkansas River in eastern Colorado.

On October 12 about 10 A. M., we broke camp and took up our line of march for the west, following the old Smoky Hill stage-route. The autumn thus far had been very mild. The great migration of the buffalo to their winter range in Texas had not yet begun, and I had some lingering doubts as to whether we might not reach our destination before the head of their column would cross our road. We had gone only about ten miles from camp, however, when I espied a solitary old bull, and instantly I was all excitement, to the great amusement of my companions. Taking an orderly from the ranks, I put spurs to my horse, and was soon in hot pursuit of this decrepit outcast. This was sport new both to my horse and myself. We were both excited and equally timid. At a range of fifty yards, or more, I emptied my revolver at the poor, tottering, old body, and a chance shot hit him and brought him to bay. It was now his turn to take up the chase. With some difficulty I recharged my weapon, and one or two more shots brought my first buffalo to earth. He was old and lean and mangy, and yet I was loath to allow one pound of his flesh to be wasted, and wanted to carry it *all* back to camp. The orderly said, with a cynical smile, "Lieutenant, he ain't no good to eat, but you might take his tongue." His smile was changed to smothered laughter when he saw me attempting to carve up the corners of the animal's mouth in order to take the tongue out between the teeth. He dismounted, and with a single cut beneath the under jaw showed me how to take out the tongue properly.

As evening came on, small groups of buffalo were seen dotting the plain. At sunrise we saw hundreds where the night before there had been only dozens. From this point on to Fort Wallace, we were never out of sight of these nomads of the "Great American Desert." From the higher points of our route, when the horizon was distant from ten to twenty miles, hundreds of thousands were visible at the same instant. They were not bunched together as cattle are, in droves, but were spread out with great regularity over the entire face of the land.

On the third day of our march, a severe snow-storm set in, accompanied by a fierce north wind—a genuine "norther." This night we were compelled to leave the road and go to the Smoky Hill River for water. We made our camp at the mouth of a small ravine that led down to the stream through the bluffs, which there form its banks. Millions of buffalo were driven before the storm, and, being prevented by the high banks of the river from crossing either above or below this point, were huddled together in a dense mass which threatened to overwhelm our little command. By placing our camp a little to one side of this living tide, and under the friendly shelter of the bluff, we passed the night in security, while the countless horde kept up its ceaseless tramp.

For six days we continued our way through this enormous herd, during the last three of which it was in constant motion across our path. I am safe in calling this a single herd, and it is impossible to approximate the millions that composed it. At times they pressed before us in such numbers as to delay the progress of our column, and often a belligerent bull would lower and shake his shaggy head at us as we passed him a few feet distant. Of course our fare was principally buffalo meat during this trip, and killing them soon ceased to be a sport.

The next year—the winter of '72 and '73—this herd, during its southward migration, extended as far west as Fort Lyon, or some seventy miles farther west than its route of previous years. It was probably driven to this course by the extension westward of settlements in Kansas and Nebraska. This was the last great migration of the southern herd of buffalo. Millions and millions were killed this season, and their hides and tongues shipped east over the Union Pacific, Kansas Pacific, and Atchison, Topeka and Santa Fé railroads, and this leads me to the short story I have to tell.

The winter had been especially severe. The entire country north of the Arkansas valley was deeply covered with snow, while the valley itself was comparatively open. The quarters in which I lived faced the south. The yard in the rear of my house was inclosed by a board fence about seven feet high, and a wide gate afforded means for entrance.

One night, in the late winter, or early spring, the region was visited by one of those terrific storms for which this section is so justly celebrated. The wind blew with a violence such as I had never before experienced, the air was filled with drifting snow, and the temperature was in the neighborhood of zero.

About the break of dawn I was awakened by my servant, who said to me: "Lieutenant, the wind blew your back gate open last night, and a buffalo has come in and taken refuge under the shelter of the fence."

It was only necessary for me to raise myself in bed and look out of the window, which was at its foot, to verify this fact. I directed that my gun and a few cartridges should be brought me, and while my servant held up the window, I, still lying in bed, gave this solitary old bull a broadside at fifty yards range. At the salutation, he started out through the gate, and before I could reload, was out of sight behind the fence, so I rolled over to resume my morning's nap.

Two or three hours later, word was brought me that I had killed the buffalo, and that his body was lying about two hundred yards back on the plain. I went out to him and took his tongue as my reward. Investigation showed that I had shot him through the lungs, and that he had been able to go thus far before succumbing to his mortal wound.

Poor, miserable, old tramp! He had evidently been driven out of the herd to die, having become a useless member of its society, and in killing him I spared him a few days of further suffering, and scored a record of buffalo-killing rarely or never paralleled.

George S. Anderson.

The White Goat and his Country

In a corner of what is occasionally termed "Our Empire of the Northwest," there lies a country of mountains and valleys where, until recently, citizens have been few. At the present time certain mines, and uncertain hopes, have gathered an eccentric population and evoked some sudden towns. The names which several of these bear are tolerably sumptuous: Golden, Oro, and Ruby, for instance; and in them dwell many colonels and judges, and people who own one suit of clothes and half a name (colored by adjuncts, such as Hurry Up Ed), and who sleep almost anywhere. These communities are brisk, sanguine, and nomadic, full of good will and crime; and in each of them you will be likely to find a weekly newspaper, and an editor who is busy writing things about the neighboring editors. The flume slants down the hill bearing water to the concentrator; buckets unexpectedly swing out from the steep pines into mid-air, sailing along their wire to the mill; little new staring shanties appear daily; somebody having trouble in a saloon upsets a lamp, and half the town goes to ashes, while the colonels and Hurry Up Eds carouse over the fireworks till morning. In a short while there are more little shanties than ever, and the burnt district is forgotten. All this is going on not far from the mountain goat, but it is a forlorn distance from the railroad; and except for the stage line which the recent mining towns have necessitated, my route to the goat country might have been too prolonged and uncertain to attempt.

I stepped down one evening from the stage, the last public conveyance I was to see, after a journey that certainly has one good side. It is completely odious; and the breed of sportsmen that takes into camp every luxury excepting, perhaps, cracked ice, will not be tempted to infest the region until civilization has smoothed its path. The path, to be sure, does not roughen until one has gone along it for twenty-eight hundred miles. You may leave New York in the afternoon, and arrive very early indeed on the fifth day at Spokane. Here the luxuries begin to lessen, and a mean once-a-day train trundles you away on a branch west of Spokane at six in the morning into a landscape that wastes into a galloping consumption. Before noon the last sick tree, the ultimate starved blade of wheat, has perished from sight, and you come to the end of all things, it would seem; a domain of wretchedness unspeakable. Not even a warm, brilliant sun can galvanize the corpse of the bare ungainly earth. The railroad goes no further,—it is not surprising,—and the stage arranges to leave before the train arrives. Thus you spend sunset and sunrise in the moribund terminal town, the inhabitants of which frankly confess that they are not staying from choice. They were floated here by a boom-wave, which left them stranded. Kindly they were, and anxious to provide the stranger with what comforts existed.

Geographically I was in the "Big Bend" country, a bulk of land looped in by the Columbia River, and highly advertised by railroads for the benefit of "those seeking homes." Fruit and grain no doubt grow somewhere in it. What I saw was a desert cracked in two by a chasm sixty-five miles long. It rained in the night, and at seven next morning, bound for Port Columbia, we wallowed northward out of town in the sweating canvas-covered stage through primeval mud. After some eighteen miles we drew out of the rain area, and from around the wheels there immediately arose and came among us a primeval dust, monstrous, shapeless, and blind. First your power of speech deserted you, then your eyesight went, and at length you became uncertain whether you were alive. Then hilarity at the sheer discomfort overtook me, and I was joined in it by a brother American; but two Jew drummers on the back seat could not understand, and seemed on the verge of tears. The landscape was entirely blotted out by the dust. Often you could not see the roadside,—if the road had any side. We may have been passing homes and fruit-trees, but I think not. I remember wondering if getting goat after all—But they proved well worth it.

Toward evening we descended into the sullen valley of the Columbia, which rushes along, sunk below the level of the desert we had crossed. High sterile hills flank its course, and with the sweeping, unfriendly speed of the stream, its bleak shores seemed a chilly place for home-seekers. Yet I blessed the change. A sight of running water once more, even of this overbearing flood, and of hills however dreary, was exhilaration after the degraded, stingy monotony of the Big Bend. The alkali trails in Wyoming do not seem paradises till you bring your memory of them here. Nor am I alone in my estimate of this impossible hole. There is a sign-post sticking up in the middle of it, that originally told the traveler it was thirty-five miles to Central Ferry. But now the traveler has retorted; and three different hand-writings on this sign-post reveal to you that you have had predecessors in your thought, comrades who shared your sorrows:

Forty-five miles to water.Seventy-five miles to wood.

And then the last word:

Two and one-half miles to hell.

Perhaps they were home-seekers.

We halted a moment at the town of Bridgeport, identified by one wooden store and an inchoate hotel. The rest may be seen upon blue-print maps, where you would suppose Bridgeport was a teeming metropolis. At Port Columbia, which we reached by a land-slide sort of road that slanted the stage over and put the twin Jew drummers in mortal fear, we slept in one of the two buildings which indicate that town. It is another important center,—in blue print,—but invisible to the naked eye. In the morning, a rope ferry floated the new stage and us travelers across the river. The Okanagon flows south from lakes and waters above the British line, and joins the Columbia here. We entered its valley at once, crossed it soon by another rope ferry, and keeping northward, with the river to the east between us and the Colville Reservation, had one good meal at noon, and entering a smaller valley, reached Ruby that evening. Here the stage left me to continue its way to Conconally, six miles further on. With the friends who had come to meet me, I ascended out of Ruby the next day over the abrupt hill westward, and passing one night out in my blankets near a hospitable but limited cabin (its flowing-haired host fed us, played us the fiddle, and would have had us sleep inside), arrived bag and baggage the fourth day from the railroad at the forks of the Methow River—the next tributary of the Columbia below the Okanagon.

Here was a smiling country, winning the heart at sight. An ample beauty was over everything Nature had accomplished in this place; the pleasant trees and clear course of the stream, a fertile soil on the levels, the slopes of the foot-hills varied and gentle, unencumbered by woods, the purple cloak of forest above these on the mountains, and rising from the valley's head a crown of white, clean frozen peaks. These are known to some as the Isabella Range and Mount Gardner, though the maps do not name them. Moreover, I heard that now I was within twenty-five miles of goats; and definite ridges were pointed out as the promised land.

Many things were said to me, first and last. I remember a ragged old trapper, lately come over the mountains from the Skagit River. Goats, did I say? On top there the goats had tangled your feet walking in the trail. He had shot two in camp for staring at him. Another accurate observer had seen three hundred on a hill just above Early Winter as he was passing by. The cabined dwellers on the Methow tied their horses to the fence and talked to me—so I had come from the East after goats, had I?—and in the store of the Man at the Forks I became something of a curiosity. Day by day I sat on the kegs of nails, or lay along the counter devoted to his dry-goods, and heard what passed. Citizens and denizens—for the Siwash with his squaws and horses was having his autumn hunt in the valley—knocked at the door to get their mail, or buy tobacco, or sell horns and fur, or stare for an hour and depart with a grunt; and the grave Man at the Forks stood behind one counter while I lay on the other, acquiring a miscellaneous knowledge. One old medical gentleman had slain all wild animals without weapons, and had been the personal friend of so many distinguished historical characters that we computed he was nineteen about the time of Bunker Hill. They were hospitable with their information, and I followed my rule of believing everything that I hear. And they were also hospitable with whatever they possessed. The memory of those distant dwellers among the mountains, young and old, is a friendly one, like the others I carry, whether of Wind or Powder Rivers, or the Yellowstone, or wherever Western trails have led me.

Yet disappointment and failure were the first things. There was all the zeal you could wish. We had wedged painfully into a severe country— twelve miles in two days, and trail-cutting between—when sickness turned us back, goatless. By this time October was almost gone, and the last three days of it went in patching up our disintegrated outfit. We needed other men and other horses; and while these were being sought, nothing was more usual than to hear "if we'd only been along with So-and-So, he saw goats" here and there, and apparently everywhere. We had, it would seem, ingeniously selected the only place where there were none. But somehow the services of So-and-So could not be procured. He had gone to town; or was busy getting his winter's meat; or his married daughter had just come to visit him, or he had married somebody else's daughter. I cannot remember the number of obstacles always lying between ourselves and So-and-So.

At length we were once more in camp on a stream named the Twispt. In the morning—new stroke of misfortune—one of us was threatened with illness, and returned to the Forks. We three, the guide, the cook, and myself, went on, finally leaving the narrow valley, and climbing four hours up a mountain at the rate of about a mile an hour. The question was, had winter come in the park above, for which we were heading? On top, we skirted a bare ridge from which everything fell precipitously away, and curving round along a steep hollow of the hill, came to an edge and saw the snow lying plentifully among the pines through which we must go down into the bottom of the park. But on the other side, where the sun came, there was little or none, and it was a most beautiful place. At the head of it was a little frozen lake fringed with tamarack, and a stream flowed down from this through scattered birches and pines, with good pasture for the horses between. The park sank at its outlet into a tall impassable cañon through which the stream joined the Twispt, miles below. It was a little lap of land clear at the top of the mountains, the final peaks and ridges of which rose all around, walling it in completely. You must climb these to be able to see into it, and the only possible approach for pack-horses was the pine-tree slant, down which we came. Of course there was no trail.

We prospected before venturing, and T——, the guide, shook his head. It was only a question of days—possibly of hours—when snow must shut the place off from the world until spring. But T—— appreciated the three thousand miles I had come for goats; and if the worst came to the worst, said he, we could "make it in" to the Forks on foot, leading the horses, and leaving behind all baggage that weighed anything. So we went down. Our animals slipped a little, the snow balling their feet; but nothing happened, and we reached the bottom and chose a camp in a clump of tamarack and pine. The little stream, passing through shadows here, ran under a lid of frozen snow easily broken, and there was plenty of wood, and on the ground only such siftings of snow as could be swept clean for the tent. The saddles were piled handily under a tree, a good fireplace was dug, we had a comfortable supper; and nothing remained but that the goats should be where they ought to be—on the ridges above the park.

I have slept more soundly; doubt and hope kept my thoughts active. Yet even so, it was pleasant to wake in the quiet and hear the bell on our horse, Duster, occasionally tankle somewhere on the hill. My watch I had forgotten to place at T——'s disposal, so he was reduced to getting the time of day from the stars. He consulted the Great Bear, and seeing this constellation at an angle he judged to indicate five o'clock, he came back into the tent, and I heard him wake the cook, who crawled out of his blankets.

"Why, it's plumb night," the cook whined.

"Make the breakfast," said T——.

I opened my eyes, and shut them immediately in despair at the darkness that I saw. Presently I heard the fire and the pans, and knew that the inevitable had come. So I got my clothes on, and we looked at my watch. It was only 4.30 A. M. T—— and the Great Bear had made half an hour's miscalculation, and the face of the cook was so grievous that I secretly laughed myself entirely awake. "Plumb night" lasted some time longer. I had leisure to eat two plates of oatmeal and maple syrup, some potato-and-onion soup, bacon, and coffee, and digest these, before dawn showed.

T—— and I left camp at 6.40 A. M. The day was a dark one. On the high peaks behind camp great mounds of cloud moved and swung, and the sky was entirely overcast. We climbed one of the lower ridges, not a hard climb nor long, but very sliding, and often requiring hands and feet to work round a ledge. From the top we could see the open country lying comfortably below and out of reach of the howling wind that cut across the top of the mountain, straight from Puget Sound, bringing all that it could carry of the damp of the Pacific. The ridges and summits that surrounded our park continually came into sight and disappeared again among the dense vapors which bore down upon them.

We went cautiously along the narrow top of crumbling slate, where the pines were scarce and stunted, and had twisted themselves into corkscrews so they might grip the ground against the tearing force of storms. We came on a number of fresh goat-tracks in the snow or the soft shale. These are the reverse of those of the mountain sheep, the V which the hoofs make having its open end in the direction the animal is going. There seemed to be several, large and small; and the perverted animals invariably chose the sharpest slant they could find to walk on, often with a decent level just beside it that we were glad enough to have. If there were a precipice and a sound flat top, they took the precipice, and crossed its face on juts that did not look as if your hat would hang on them. In this I think they are worse than the mountain sheep, if that is possible. Certainly they do not seem to come down into the high pastures and feed on the grass levels as the sheep will.

T—— and I hoped we should find a bunch, but that was not to be, in spite of the indications. As we continued, I saw a singular-looking stone lying on a little ledge some way down the mountain ahead. I decided it must be a stone, and was going to speak of it, when the stone moved, and we crouched in the slanting gravel. T—— had been making up his mind it was a stone. The goat turned his head our way, but did not rise. He was two hundred yards across a split in the mountain, and the wind blowing hard. T—— wanted me to shoot, but I did not dare to run such a chance. I have done a deal of missing at two hundred yards, and much nearer, too. So I climbed, or crawled, out of sight, keeping any stone or little bush between me and the goat, till I got myself where a buttress of rock hid me, and then I ran along the ridge and down and up the scoop in it made by the split of the mountain, and so came cautiously to where I could peer over and see the goat lying turned away from me, with his head commanding the valley. He was on a tiny shelf of snow, beside him was one small pine, and below that the rock fell away steeply into the gorge. Ought I to have bellowed at him, and at least have got him on his legs? I know it would have been more honorable. He looked white, and huge, and strange; and somehow I had a sense of personality about him more vivid than any since I watched my first silver-tip lift a rotten log, and, sitting on his hind legs, make a breakfast on beetles, picking them off the log with one paw.

I fired, aiming behind the goat's head. He did not rise, but turned his head round. The white bead of my Lyman sight had not showed well against the white animal, and I thought I had missed him. Then I fired again, and he rolled very little—six inches—and lay quiet. He could not have been more than fifty yards away, and my first shot had cut through the back of his neck and buried itself in mortal places, and the second in his head merely made death instantaneous. Shooting him after he had become alarmed might have lost him over the edge; even if a first shot had been fatal, it could not have been fatal soon enough. Two struggles on that snow would have sent him sliding through space. As it was, we had a steep, unsafe scramble down through the snow to where he lay stretched out on the little shelf by the tree.

He was a fair-sized billy, and very heavy. The little lifting and shoving we had to do in skinning him was hard work. The horns were black, slender, slightly spreading, curved backward, pointed, and smooth. They measured six inches round the base, and the distance from one point to the other, measured down one horn, along the skull, and up the other, was twenty-one and a half inches. The hoofs were also black and broad and large, wholly unlike a tame goat's. The hair was extraordinarily thick, long, and of a weather-beaten white; the eye large and deep-brown.

I had my invariable attack of remorse on looking closely at the poor harmless old gentleman, and wondered what achievement, after all, could be discerned in this sort of surprise and murder. We did not think of securing any of his plentiful fat, but with head and hide alone climbed back up the ticklish slant, hung the trophies on a tree in a gap on the camp side of the ridge, and continued our hunt. It was not ten o'clock yet, and we had taken one hour to skin the goat. We now hunted the higher ridges behind camp until 1 P. M., finding tracks that made it seem as if a number of goats must be somewhere near by. But the fog came down and shut everything out of sight; moreover, the wind on top blew so that we could not have seen had it been clear.

We returned to camp, and found it greatly improved. The cook had carpentered an important annex to the tent. By slanting pine-logs against a ridge-pole and nailing them, he had built a room, proof against wind and rain, and in it a table. One end was against the opening of the tent, the other at the fire. The arrangement was excellent, and timely also. The storm revived during the night, and it rained fitfully. The roar of the wind coming down from the mountain into our park sounded like a Niagara, and its approach was tremendous. We had built up a barrier of pine-brush, and this, with a clump of trees, sheltered us well enough; but there were wild moments when the gust struck us, and the tent shuddered and strained, until that particular breeze passed on with a diminishing roar down the cañon.

The next morning the rain kept us from making an early start, and we did not leave camp until eight. Now and then a drizzle fell from the mist, and the banks of clouds were still driving across the higher peaks, but during the day the sun slowly got the better of them. Again we saw a solitary goat, this time far below down the ridge we had chosen. Like the sheep, these animals watch the valley. There is no use in attempting to hunt them from there. Their eyes are watchful and keen, and the chances are that if you are working up from below and see a goat on the hill, he will have been looking at you for some time. Once he is alarmed, ten minutes will be enough for him to put a good many hours of climbing between himself and you. His favorite trick is to remain stock-still, watching you till you pass out of his sight behind something, and then he makes off so energetically that when you see him next he will be on some totally new mountain. But his intelligence does not seem to grasp more than the danger from below. While he is steadfastly on the alert against this, it apparently does not occur to him that anything can come down upon him. Consequently from above you may get very near before you are noticed. The chief difficulty is the noise of falling stones your descent is almost sure to make. The character of these mountain-sides is such that even with the greatest care in stepping we sent a shower rattling down from time to time. We had a viciously bad climb. We went down through tilted funnels of crag, avoiding jumping off places by crossing slides of brittle slate and shale, hailing a dead tree as an oasis. And then we lost count, and T— came unexpectedly on the goat, which was up and away and was shot by T—— before I could get a sight of him. I had been behind some twenty yards, both of us supposing we had to go considerably further. T— was highly disgusted. "To think of me managing such a botch as that," he said, "when you've come so far"; and he wanted me to tell the people that I had shot the goat myself. He really cared more than I did.

This goat was also a billy, and larger than the first. We sat skinning him where he had fallen at the edge of a grove of tamarack, and T— conversed about the royal family of England. He remarked that he had always rather liked "that chap Lorne."

I explained to him that "that chap Lorne" had made himself ridiculous forever at the Queen's Jubilee. Then, as T— did not know, I told him how the marquis had insisted on riding in the procession upon a horse, against which the Prince of Wales, aware of the tame extent of his horsemanship, had warned him. In the middle of the pageant, the Queen in her carriage, the crowned heads of Europe escorting her on horseback, and the whole world looking on—at this picturesque moment, Lorne fell off. I was not sure that T—— felt fully how inappropriate a time this was for a marquis to tumble from his steed.

"I believe the Queen sent somebody," I continued.

"Where?" said T——.

"To him. She probably called the nearest king and said: 'Frederick, Lorne's off. Go and see if he's hurt.'"

"'And if he ain't hurt, *hurt him*,'" said T——, completing her Majesty's thought.

On the Slide-Rock.
Photographed from nature by William H. Seward, Jr. From Forest and Stream.

This second billy seemed to me twice the size of a domestic goat. He was certainly twice the weight. His hide alone weighed thirty pounds, as far as one could determine by balancing it against weights that we knew, such as a sack of flour or sugar. But I distrust the measurements of wild animals made by guesswork on a mountain-top during the enthusiastic state of the hunter's mind which follows at once upon a lucky shot. Therefore, I can positively vouch for this only, that all the goats which I have seen struck me as being larger and heavier animals than the goat of civilization. After all, the comparison is one into which we are misled by the name. This is an antelope; and though, through certain details of his costume, he is able to masquerade as a goat, it must be remembered that he is of a species wholly distinct.

We took the web tallow, and the tallow of one kidney. The web was three quarters of an inch thick.

Neither elk, nor any animal I have seen, except bear, has such quantities of fat, and I do not think even a bear has a thicker hide. On the rump it was as thick as the sole of my boot, and the masses of hair are impenetrable to anything but modern firearms. An arrow might easily stick harmless; and I am told that carnivorous animals who prey upon the deer in these mountains respectfully let the goat alone. Besides his defensive armor, he is an ugly customer in attack. He understands the use of his thin, smooth horns, and, driving them securely into the belly of his enemy, jumps back and leaves him a useless, ripped-open sack. Male and female have horns of much the same size; and in taking a bite out of one of either sex, as T—— said, a mountain lion would get only a mouthful of hair.

But modern firearms have come to be appreciated by the wild animals; and those which were once unquestionably dangerous to pioneers, now retreat before the Winchester rifle. Only a bear with cubs to defend remains formidable.

I said this to T——, who told me a personal experience that tends to destroy even this last chance for the sportsman to be doughty. T—— came on a bear and cubs in the spring, and of course they made off, but his dog caught and held one little cub which cried out like a child—and its contemptible mama hurried straight on and away.

Not so a goat mama of which T—— also told me. Some prospectors came on a bunch of goats when the kids were young enough to be caught. One of the men captured a kid, and was walking off with it, when the mother took notice and charged furiously down on him. He flew by in ignominious sight of the whole camp with the goat after him, till he was obliged to drop the kid, which was then escorted back to its relatives by its most competent parent.

Yet no room for generalizing is here. We cannot conclude that the *Ursus* family fails to think blood as thick as other people do. These two incidents merely show that the race of bears is capable of producing unmaternal females, while, on the other hand, we may expect occasionally to find in a nanny-goat a Mother of the Gracchi.

I wished to help carry the heavy hide of the second billy; but T—— inflicted this upon himself, "every step to camp," he insisted, "for punishment at disappointing you." The descent this day had been bad enough, taking forty minutes for some four hundred yards. But now we were two hours getting up, a large part of the way on hands and knees. I carried the two rifles and the glass, going in front to stamp some sort of a trail in the sliding rocks, while T—— panted behind me, bearing the goat-hide on his back.

Our next hunt was from seven till four, up and down, in the presence of noble and lonely mountains. The straight peaks which marshal round the lake of Chelan were in our view near by, beyond the valley of the Twispt, and the whole Cascade range rose endlessly, and seemed to fill the world. Except in Switzerland, I have never seen such an unbroken area of mountains. And all this beauty going begging, while each year our American citizens of the East, more ignorant of their own country and less identified with its soil than any race upon earth, herd across the sea to the tables d'hôte they know by heart! But this is wandering a long way from goats, of which this day we saw none.

A gale set in after sunset. This particular afternoon had been so mellow, the sun had shone so clear from a stable sky, that I had begun to believe the recent threats of winter were only threats, and that we had some open time before us still. Next morning we waked in midwinter, the flakes flying thick and furious over a park that was no longer a pasture, but a blind drift of snow. We lived in camp, perfectly comfortable.

Down at the Forks I had had made a rough imitation of a Sibley stove. All that its forger had to go on was my unprofessional and inexpert description, and a lame sketch in pencil; but he succeeded so well that the hollow iron cone and joints of pipe he fitted together turned out most efficient. The sight of the apparatus packed on a horse with the panniers was whimsical, and until he saw it work I know that T— despised it. After that, it commanded his respect. All this stormy day it roared and blazed, and sent a lusty heat throughout the tent. T— cleaned the two goat-heads, and talked Shakspere and Thackeray to me. He quoted Henry the Fourth, and regretted that Thackeray had not more developed the character of George Warrington. Warrington was the *man* in the book. When night came the storm was gone.

By eight the next morning we had sighted another large solitary billy. But he had seen us down in the park from his ridge. He had come to the edge, and was evidently watching the horses. If not quick-witted, the goat is certainly wary; and the next time we saw him he had taken himself away down the other side of the mountain, along a spine of rocks where approach was almost impossible. We watched his slow movements through the glass, and were both reminded of a bear. He felt safe, and was stepping deliberately along, often stopping, often walking up some small point and surveying the scenery. He moved in an easy, rolling fashion, and turned his head importantly. Then he lay down in the sun, but saw us on our way to him, and bounced off. We came to the place where he had jumped down sheer twenty feet at least. His hoof-tracks were on the edge, and in the gravel below the heavy scatter he made in landing; and then,—hasty tracks round a corner of rock, and no more goat that day.

I had become uneasy about the weather. It was all sunshine again, and though our first goat was irretrievably gone, we had the afternoon before us. Nevertheless, when I suggested we should spend it in taking the shoes off the horses, so they might be able to walk homeward without falling in the snow, T— thought it our best plan. We wanted to find a bunch of goats now, nannies and kids, as well as billies. It had been plain that these ridges here contained very few, and those all hermits; males who from age, or temperament, or disappointment in love, had retired from society, and were spending the remainder of their days in a quiet isolation and whatever is the goat equivalent for reading Horace. It was well enough to have begun with these philosophers, but I wanted new specimens.

We were not too soon. A new storm had set in by next morning, and the unshod horses made their journey down the mountain, a most odious descent for man and beast, in the sliding snow. But down on the Twispt it was yet only autumn, with no snow at all. This was a Monday, the 7th of November, and we made haste to the Forks, where I stopped a night to read a large, accumulated mail, and going on at once, overtook my outfit, which had preceded me on the day before.

Our new camp—and our last one—was up the Methow, twenty-three miles above the Forks, in a straight line. Here the valley split at right angles against a tall face of mountain, and each way the stream was reduced to a brook one could cross afoot. The new valley became steep and narrow almost at once, and so continued to the divide between Columbia water and tributaries of the Skagit. We lived comfortably in an old cabin built by prospectors. The rain filtered through the growing weeds and sand on the roof and dropped on my head in bed; but not much, and I was able to steer it off by a rubber blanket. And of course there was no glass in the windows; but to keep out wind and wet we hung gunny sacks across those small holes, and the big stone fireplace was magnificent.

By ten next morning T—— and I saw "three hundred" goats on the mountain opposite where we had climbed. Just here I will risk a generalization. When a trapper tells you he has seen so many hundred head of game, he has not counted them, but he believes what he says. The goats T—— and I now looked at were a mile away in an air-line, and they seemed numberless. The picture which the white, slightly moving dots made, like mites on a cheese, inclined one to a large estimate of them, since they covered the whole side of a hill. The more we looked the more we found; besides the main army there were groups, caucuses, families sitting apart over some discourse too intimate for the general public; and beyond these single animals could be discerned, moving, gazing, browsing, lying down.

"Megod and Begod," said T—— (he occasionally imitated a brogue for no hereditary reason), "there's a hundred thousand goats!"

"Let's count'em," I suggested, and we took the glasses. There were thirty-five.

We found we had climbed the wrong hill, and the day was too short to repair this error. Our next excursion, however, was successful. The hill where the goats were was not two miles above camp,—you could have seen the animals from camp but for the curve in the cañon,—yet we were four hours and a half climbing the ridge, in order to put ourselves above them. It was a hard climb, entirely through snow after the first. On top the snow came at times considerably above the knees. But the judicious T—— (I have never hunted with a more careful and thorough man) was right in the route he had chosen, and after we had descended again to the edge of the snow, we looked over a rock, and saw, thirty yards below us, the nanny and kid for which we had been aiming. I should have said earlier that the gathering of yesterday had dispersed during the night, and now little bunches of three and four goats could be seen up and down the cañon. We were on the exact ground they had occupied, and their many tracks were plain. My first shot missed—thirty yards!—and as nanny and kid went bounding by on the hill below, I knocked her over with a more careful bullet, and T—— shot the kid. The little thing was not dead when we came up, and at the sight of us it gave a poor little thin bleat that turns me remorseful whenever I think of it. We had all the justification that any code exacts. We had no fresh meat, and among goats the kid alone is eatable; and I justly desired specimens of the entire family.

We carried the whole kid to camp, and later its flesh was excellent. The horns of the nanny, as has been said before, are but slightly different from those of the male. They are, perhaps, more slender, as is also the total makeup of the animal. In camp I said to T—— that I desired only one more of those thirty-five goats, a billy; and that if I secured him the next day, that should be the last. Fortune was for us. We surprised a bunch of several. They had seen me also, and I was obliged to be quick. This resulted in some shots missing, and in two, perhaps three, animals going over ledges with bullets in them, leaving safe behind the billy I wanted. His conduct is an interesting example of the goat's capacity to escape you and die uselessly, out of your reach.

I had seen him reel at my first shot, but he hurried around a corner, and my attention was given to others. As I went down, I heard a shot, and came round the corner on T——, who stood some hundred yards further along the ledge beside a goat. T—— had come on him lying down. He had jumped up and run apparently unhurt, and T—— had shot him just as he reached the end of the ledge. Beyond was a fall into inaccessible depths. Besides T——'s shot we found two of mine— one clean through from the shoulder—the goat had faced me when I fired first—to the ham, where the lead was flat against the bone. This goat was the handsomest we had, smaller than the other males, but with horns of a better shape, and with hair and beard very rich and white. Curiously enough, his lower jaw between the two front teeth had been broken a long time ago, probably from some fall. Yet this accident did not seem to have interfered with his feeding, for he was in excellent plump condition.

This completely satisfied me, and I willingly decided to molest no more goats. I set neither value nor respect on numerical slaughter. One cannot expect Englishmen to care whether American big game is exterminated or not; that Americans should not care is a disgrace. The pervading spirit of the far West as to game, as to timber, as to everything that a true American should feel it his right to use and his duty to preserve for those coming after, is—"What do I care, so long as it lasts my time?"

There remain a few observations to make, and then I have said the little that I know about goats. Their horns are not deciduous, so far at least as I could learn, and the books say this also. But I read a somewhat inaccurate account of the goat's habits in winter-time. It was stated that at that season, like mountain sheep, he descends and comes into the valleys. This does not seem to be the case. He does not depend upon grass, if indeed he eats grass at all. His food seems to be chiefly the short, almost lichen-like moss that grows on the faces and at the base of the rocks and between them in the crevices. The community of goats I watched was feeding; afterward, when on the spot where they had been, I found there was no grass growing anywhere near, and signs pointed to its having been the moss and rock plants that they had been eating. None of the people in the Methow country spoke of seeing goats come out of the mountains during winter. I have not sufficient data to make the assertion, but I am inclined to believe that the goat keeps consistently to the hills, whatever the season may be, and in this differs from the mountain sheep as he differs in appearance, temperament, and in all characteristics excepting the predilection for the inclined plane; and in this habit he is more vertical than the sheep.

Lest the region I hunted in may have remained vague to Eastern readers, it is as well to add that in an air-line I was probably some thirty miles below the British border, and some hundred and twenty east of Puget Sound.

Owen Wister.

A Day with the Elk

Early in September of 1890, we were in camp in the northern part of Colorado, an easy day's ride from the Wyoming line. Our party, eight in all, consisted of myself, three friends, three packers, and a cook. We had been out nearly a month, and after the first week our success had been good. We were taking life very easily—hunting a little, fishing now and then, and doing a great deal of healthy "lying round camp."

Game was very plentiful. There were black-tail and elk all around us. The antelope, than whom the ammunition manufacturer has no truer friend, were within easy reach. One of the party had bagged two bears, and a packer had found a dead one, whose fore-paws and ears were sufficiently preserved to be worth a $10 bounty to the finder.

The outfit with two exceptions was content. Our cook, having surreptitiously drunk all the whisky, was struggling with an increasing thirst provoked by an empty demi-john. My cup of happiness, unlike the cook's, had never been emptied, but it was far from full. I had not shot an elk. They were all round us, and had been for a fortnight. I had hunted them alone and in company. I had had many chances at young bulls, but had hitherto held my hand, waiting in vain for a good head. We had plenty of meat—a condition of things forbidding useless slaughter. Spike bulls and cows were therefore sacred, and seemed to know it, for they gave me every chance to take advantage of their youthful inexperience or sex. Twice I had stumbled on a large band in timber. I had heard the musical challenges of the young bulls answered by the patriarch, with his squealing whistle ending in a deep grunt of conscious superiority. The young bulls were provokingly plentiful—but the patriarchs always invisible. Of course every other member of the outfit saw the "biggest bull yet" whenever I happened to be absent. Each of my three friends had a good head or two to his score, and their accounts were closed. Our time was nearly up, and I began to despair of getting what I wanted. For two days I sulked in my tent, and then one morning Robert Bruce's historic spider fell into my lap from the tent-pole, and I arose and went forth for a last try.

Our camp was by a stream in an aspen grove, on the edge of one of those open spaces which, be they large or small, are known in Colorado as parks. Behind us to the south lay heavily timbered ridges, alternating with little valleys full of shade-trees, long, sweet grass, and pleasant brooks. There, I thought, was as good a place as any in which to find the "faultless monster that the world ne'er saw," and thither I accordingly went.

It was about noon when I started, and my intention was to work away to the south, and then hunt back to camp toward evening. I know that there are those who say that if you want to kill game you must get up early. They are perfectly right, and I agree with them entirely. But there are others who maintain with equal truth that toward sundown is the best time. One time is as good as the other, and inasmuch as an empty belly and the dark before the dawn are bitter things to me, and to be avoided if possible, I prefer the evening shooting. So, fortified with a good night's rest, and a breakfast calculated to last me till the morrow, I set forth alone and on foot.

In hunting, as in most cases where real work is to be done, one is best alone. Two people are apt to talk just at the wrong time. And even if you do not talk at all, four feet make—of necessity—more noise than two, and two bodies are easier seen than one. I left my horse behind, because I did not wish to burden myself with an extra responsibility. A horse can be a dreadful nuisance. You may want to go where he cannot, and so you must either leave him tied up somewhere, or else suit your way to his. Again, you lose valuable time in dismounting and tying up, before stalking or shooting your game. And both time and temper suffer when you can't find the place where you left your horse. Some men have the true woodsman's instinct, and never get lost or turned round. These are fortunate beings, and worthy of respectful admiration. But woe to him who, unendowed by nature with their gifts, seeks to imitate them. For my part I have always had quite enough to do to keep my head and feet agreed as to the direction of camp. Any extra strain, such as the necessity of looking for a mislaid horse, is sure to cause a disagreement between the members, and so bring on a catastrophe.

I had been out several hours. It was getting on toward evening, and I was well on my way home. There was no lack of elk in the neighborhood, for my more fortunate friends had proved that they were easy to find. I could see that bands had roved that very morning over the country through which my path lay. I could see where some great bull had thrashed the young sapling with his horns till the tender bark was stripped off, or hung in long, wet ribbons from the wounded tree. And in the pools where the big fellows had wallowed, the mud had scarce settled. In places the grass was trampled and littered as if by a bunch of cattle. The "sign" was plentiful and fresh. Still I heard no whistle, nor saw a living thing, save now and then when a big-eyed black-tail doe would gaze at me with mild wonder until she got my wind, and then away she would bounce through the timber, followed by her startled fawn.

But the shadows were getting longer and the air cooler; the sun was going rapidly down hill. I knew that now was the time when the elk were sure to be moving down out of the timber for their evening feed in the open glades. I was making my way quietly along a little stream, whose timbered banks afforded good cover, and at the same time a view of the small parks running up to the wooded ridges on either side. Suddenly my heart went to my throat, and I dropped in my tracks. There—to the left and within a few yards of me—was a cow coming down through the timber to drink. Close behind her was another cow, and then a young spike bull. I lay still and breathless, praying to all the gods that the band, which I felt sure was behind, might pass my hiding-place. There would surely be a big bull or two among them, and at that distance if I missed—. I was already thinking whether the neck or the shoulder was the best chance. The cow bent her head to the water, and began to drink. Her two companions paused on the brink. Nothing else showed. The cow raised her dripping muzzle. I was so near that I could hear the drops tinkle as they fell back into the stream. And then a puff of wind, soft as a sigh, fanned my cheek, and with a snort and a bound the two cows and their youthful escort vanished back into the wood. They had got my wind, for see me they could not, and no log could have lain more still.

Then arose a mighty trampling on the other side of the stream. The trio had evidently rejoined the band, startling them by their sudden retreat. I crept across the stream, and crawled through the thicket to spy out the land beyond. A thick, low clump of trees thrust itself like a venomous green tongue out into the open park which stretched away in front of me to the right and left. Beyond the park was a heavily wooded ridge, whither I felt sure the band had gone. But no—not all! Further on, at the extreme end of the green tongue of timber, in full view and broadside on, stood a young bull. He was evidently the last of the herd. He stood gazing about him as if he wondered what had startled the others, and why they had left him so unceremoniously. What a picture he made, as he stood outlined against the green hillside, turning his lordly head slowly from side to side with watchful eye and spreading nostril! I had seen plenty as good as he, and had held my hand. But then it might be my last chance. He was only a ten-pointer. But I had gone home so often empty handed, and he was only seventy or eighty yards away. Instinctively my rifle went to my shoulder, my finger pressed the trigger, the elk plunged forward and fell on his knees. As he struggled to rise, I shot him again. And then—what are mere words to describe what I felt! On my left, beyond the accursed green tongue, went with a rush a great band of cows and calves. And in their very midst rolled the great-grandfather of all the elk in the State of Colorado,—a perfect monster! His back was as broad and as yellow as the Tiber in spring. His horns were as thick as a strong man's arm, and spread like the branches of an oak. Across the park and up the hill he went, his wives and children thronging round him so close that I could not shoot for fear of doing useless harm. Up and over the ridge and into the timber he went, and I saw him no more. It was all over in a moment; then I remembered the young bull I had shot, and went and sat down by him. I expressed my profound regret for what had occurred, and explained how it had all happened. His grandpapa should have shown himself a moment sooner, or at least should have had the decency to separate himself from the ladies when running away. And then, having performed the necessary rites, I left him where he lay, and started for camp to get a packer and a horse.

My way lay over the very ridge the elk had crossed in their flight. Thinking that I might get another chance at the big fellow, I went carefully along, keeping a sharp lookout ahead. For about an hour I kept on through the woods. It was getting dark fast, but I was very near home, and could see the great park on the edge of which our camp lay. As I walked, I could hear from time to time the whistling of bulls on all sides; some far off, and some seemingly quite near at hand. In crossing a large open patch of burnt timber, I was stopped by a very loud whistle close in front; and, on creeping up, saw on the far edge of the clearing three bulls standing. They were between me and camp, and not two hundred yards away. They seemed to hear or see me, but stood perfectly still, probably mistaking me in the dusk for one of their number. One was a big fellow, I could see, as he stood out against the sky. What horns he had! The failing light made him seem gigantic. I crawled on till within easy range, and still he never moved. He was standing breast on, apparently watching me. Aiming for where his great shaggy throat joined his broad breast I fired. The rifle blazed out in the dusk; the elk gave a bound, and turned his quarter toward me; the other two dashed off into the woods. Again I fired; this time for his shoulder. The flash of the rifle half blinded me for an instant, but I could see that he was down. I started for him at a run. Up he got, and went lurching heavily down hill toward camp. I was now quite close to him, and fired once more. Again he fell, but, the slope aiding him, he struggled up and went stumbling along. There was no need of another shot. He was nearly spent, and my only thought was to get him as near camp as possible. Forgetting all about the danger of going too near a wounded elk, I was close at his quarter, hurling sticks and stones at him to drive him home, as one would an ox. The hill was steep; my second shot had broken his shoulder; he pitched rather than walked down the slope; and finally fell forward in a heap and breathed his last.

He was not the monster I had lost, but he was a grand big one; as big as any we had killed on that trip. I had what I wanted at last, and having marked well the spot where he lay, I heaved a sigh of satisfaction and started for camp.

In half an hour I was stowing away a well-earned supper, and fighting my battle over again for the benefit of all who chose to listen. About nine o'clock I went back with two packers and a horse to where my prize lay stiff and cold. By the light of a roaring fire we cut him up, and then, loading the horse with what we wanted, we left the remainder for the bears and coyotes, and betook ourselves to camp.

Two days later I had the melancholy satisfaction of assisting at the decapitation of the monster who had escaped me. I devoutly believe it was the same elk, and though of course I cannot swear to his identity, yet I am sure he must have been a full brother to old Yellow Back. My friend had stalked and shot him while superintending the luncheons, siestas and gambols of his numerous family. When I saw him I groaned in spirit, and congratulated the lucky sportsman. We took only his head, for he was too much married by far to be good eating. His mighty body was left as a *memento mori* to the valiant bull who succeeded him in the affections of his widows and offspring.

Winthrop Chanler.

Old Times in the Black Hills.

In the spring of '75 I found myself one of a party of six occupying a rude but strongly fortified stockade on French Creek, in the Black Hills, almost under the shadow of Calamity Peak, and not far from where Custer City was afterward built.

I had left Denver the previous fall, quite a tenderfoot, and, like Lord Lovel of milk-white steed fame, wanting "strange countries for to see," I determined to join a party that I heard was outfitting at Cheyenne to go into the Black Hills upon a hunting and prospecting tour, under the guidance of old California Joe, one of the most noted scouts and hunters in the West. At this time the presence of gold in the Black Hills was hardly known, and the country; being an Indian reservation, had not even been explored by white men, or surveyed by the government. The plans of the party in question suited my ideas exactly, and I soon found myself on the back of a "cayuse," followed by a good stout packhorse, equipped for a journey of several months, *en route* to Cheyenne, probably one hundred miles due north. After two days of hard riding I reached Cheyenne, and found that the party had started two days before, intending to cross the Platte River at Fort Laramie, another hundred miles north. Undaunted, I pushed on without delay, not even stopping to take a shot at any of the numerous bands of antelope that continually crossed my path. I reached the post the second day, only to learn from a "bull-whacker"—I dared not disclose my purpose to the officers—that the party I was looking for had been turned back by the troops as trespassers on Indian territory, and were supposed to have gone in the direction of Fort Fetterman. Though somewhat disheartened, I lost no time in following them, and soon rode into their camp, after dark, in a blinding snow-storm.

My welcome was anything but cordial. They regarded my story that I, a tenderfoot, had ridden through from Denver in four days to join them as suspicious, and believed, as I afterward ascertained, that I had been sent out from the post to spy upon their movements. As I rode into camp I noticed they were just finishing supper. During the argument that followed my arrival and proposition to join them, I observed a large, powerfully built man, dressed in buckskin, seated apart from the rest. He was eating the meat from a section of ribs he had scraped out from among the coals and ashes. He took no part in the conversation until, in answer to a question, I stated that I was a Kentuckian. At this he rose and settled the matter by saying that if I was a Kentuckian he would vouch for my honesty of purpose, and that I would stand fire in the scrimmages that we were certain to have with the Sioux. This was California Joe, who for years had been chief of scouts with General Custer. He afterward informed me that he was from near Danville, Kentucky, that his name was Mose Milner, and that he had gone West in the forties. I mention this from the fact that I have since read an account referring to him as one of the most noted characters in the West, whose life was surrounded by mystery, as he always refused to tell his real name or whence he came.

After waiting a couple of days for the river to fall, we forded just above the junction of the Laramie and the Platte. I came very near losing my packhorse and entire outfit, one horse being drowned in the treacherous quicksands in spite of our strenuous efforts to rescue him. At the end of a two weeks' journey through the best game country I ever hunted in, we entered the Black Hills proper, through Red Cañon, the place where the Metz party and many prospectors *en route* to the new Eldorado were afterward killed by the Indians. Old Joe had several opportunities to verify his good opinion of my ability to stand fire, as we were attacked by roving bands of Sioux at Alkali Springs, Hat Creek, and Red Cañon. Our first action was to erect a couple of log cabins and surround them with a strong stockade, with a bastion at each corner. We spent the entire winter here, feeling secure of our ability to stand off any bands of Indians that might attempt to dislodge us. We were utterly oblivious of the fact that the Indians had reported our presence, and that the government had sent out troops from both Red Cloud and Spotted Tail agencies to bring us in; one command, under Lieutenant Mix, returning after several weeks' unsuccessful search with a large percentage of the men suffering from frozen extremities.

In the early part of the winter game was plentiful; it was a perfect hunter's paradise, it being necessary only to sit in the stockade gate and shoot deer coming down to water. We frequently had eight or ten carcasses swung to our corner-poles, and did not deign to eat other than the choice pieces, throwing the remainder over the stockade walls to attract wolves at night. These we shot for their pelts. In the early spring the Indians coming in for "tepee" poles burned the country for miles around us, and quite a little jaunt became necessary to find game. We generally took turn about at supplying the table with meat, and it eventually proved anything but a sinecure.

On one such hunt I met with a rather curious misadventure. It being my turn to replenish the larder, which, by the way, had for several weeks contained absolutely nothing but meat,—not even coffee,—I placed a rawhide hackamore and a pack on "Coffee," an extra bronco I had bought, filled my pouch with a good supply of jerked bear-meat, and calling two of the dogs,—Kentuck, a greyhound, and Maida, a deerhound,—I struck out just as the sun was peeping over the hills. I decided to go to the foot-hills in the direction of Buffalo Gap, in the hope of finding antelope in some of the valleys. Noon found me near Point of Rocks and still tramping, "Coffee" trailing leisurely along, at times dropping entirely out of sight while looking for unburned grass, then whinnying and scampering after me full tilt, like a boy just out from school. I had seen several deer and a couple of sheep, but none within range.

Here I came upon some cottontail rabbits, the first and only ones I ever saw in that part of the country. They were not frightened by my presence, evidently never having been disturbed by man. I tried a shot at one very near me, and as I was using 107 grains of powder, entirely overshot him. Although the smoke of the gun reached him, he did not budge an inch; a second shot literally scattered him to the winds. The dogs, returning at this point, quickly despatched several.

Leaving "Coffee" in the valley, I decided to give up antelope and take my chances on deer and sheep on the mountain-side. When about winded from my exertions, I dropped upon a fallen pine, somewhat disgusted with my ill luck. Presently I heard the distinct bark of a deer very close to me. Peering cautiously from behind a huge granite boulder that obstructed my view ahead, my heart beat faster in an incipient buck-fever, for not sixty yards from me, on a small plateau, stood a big buck, while at his feet lay a doe. His head was slightly turned toward me, his nostrils were quivering and distended, and he looked as if prepared to bound away. He was evidently alarmed by the noise of the dogs I had left in the cañon, which were now making their way up the steep sides of the mountain. He seemed utterly oblivious of my presence; and there was a look of proud defiance in his eye that gave him a most noble, majestic appearance as he stood impatiently striking the hard ground with his fore foot. I had long been anxious to kill two deer with one shot, a feat I had twice seen accomplished by others, so I paused a minute with rifle at full cock, hoping the doe would arise alongside of him. I had not long to wait; his note of warning aroused her, and she jumped to her feet.

Taking a quick aim just back of his shoulder, I fired. As soon as the smoke cleared from in front of my eyes, I saw him still standing erect; he shook his antlers, paused a moment, then rearing to his full height he pitched forward upon his head, apparently stone dead. Forgetting in the excitement of the moment to take a second shot at the doe, which was now bounding off seemingly uninjured, I ran exultingly forward to the buck, dropping my rifle on the edge of the plateau as I reached for my hunting-knife to cut his throat. To my amazement he bounded to his feet and made straight at me, meeting my advance with a charge as sudden as it was unexpected. His onslaught was irresistible, and striking me squarely, he sent me whirling heels over head, fortunately landing me near my rifle, for in reaching for my knife I discovered it was missing. Scrambling to my feet, I arose with my rifle in my hand, and not a minute too soon, for the now thoroughly enraged buck was upon me, with eyes gleaming like coals of fire. I clubbed my gun and struck at his lowered head, hitting the bur of his antlers; and the rifle flew out of my hands, broken in two at the grip. I grasped him by the antlers, and the tussle we then had would have been an interesting and thrilling one to a spectator. I myself would have much preferred the rôle of spectator to that of participant, but unfortunately I had no choice in the matter.

The dogs, now coming up, fortunately divided his attention. Kentuck promptly seized him by the ear and hung on bravely, notwithstanding the sharp hoofs of the buck were cutting him frightfully at each stroke of his deadly fore feet; Maida, in the mean time, was unable to secure a hold that would assist us. In my efforts to hold his head down I slipped and fell, and buck, dogs, and myself mingled in a confused heap. As I fell I lost my hold on the antlers and scrambled for my mutilated rifle; but before I found whether it could be used or not, the buck lunged forward, falling with Kentuck beneath him. It was his last effort; he was dead. Completely winded from my continued and violent exertions in the light air,—being almost up to timber-line,—I sank upon the ground, and could not refrain from smiling at the forlorn appearance we presented.

Blowing like porpoises, their tongues lolling out, covered with blood from their own and the buck's wounds, the dogs lay extended at full length. An examination revealed that Kentuck's mouth was split almost to his ears, and there was a hole in his abdomen from which his entrails protruded, besides several minor cuts. Maida was more bloody than hurt, having lost several patches of skin, and hair enough to pad a saddle. As for myself, my antelope-skin shirt and overalls were ripped and bloody, one sole was torn from my heavy hunting-boots, elbows and knees were skinned by the sharp ledges of slate and loose quartz scattered about, and I had a badly cut lip and several loose teeth. I considered my greatest injury the damage to my rifle. It was one that I had made to order by Freund, of Denver, being a 45-caliber, heavy octagon barrel, Springfield needle-gun movement, with set triggers and curled maple pistol-grip stock. I considered this the best all-round sporting-rifle I had ever owned. I was three hundred miles from a gunsmith, virtually unarmed, and carrying my life in my hand.

An examination of the dead buck proved him indeed a grand specimen. He had eight points to each antler, and their condition and his numerous scars proved conclusively that he had ever been willing to defend his title as monarch of the woods. I never would have believed that any deer could attain so large a size, and though I have hunted them from Arizona to Montana, I have never seen his equal either as to size or condition. This fact determined me to carry him into camp whole; in fact, I had no other alternative, being without a knife. I found the task of cutting his throat with sharp pieces of slate a tedious one indeed, and I had a terrible time getting the carcass on "Coffee," who, although the best packhorse I ever saw, had never overcome his horror of a dead animal, and did not even relish the rabbits I had strapped on him at noon. It may seem a simple thing, but I found loading that buck without assistance one of the hardest tasks I ever undertook, and more than once was on the point of giving it up. However, my desire to substantiate my claim of having bagged the largest deer of any of the party sharpened my wits. Snubbing "Coffee's" nose up tight against a tree growing at the base of a ledge on to which I had succeeded in dragging and rolling the carcass, I blindfolded him with my hunting-shirt, and then managed to roll the buck on the pack from the ledge.

By the time this was accomplished, the sun was sinking behind the mountain. Returning slowly to the valley, no course was left me but to camp for the night, for I was at least fifteen miles from the stockade. I may have been a fit subject for the Society for the Prevention of Cruelty to Animals, but "Coffee" spent that night in the embrace of a "diamond hitch," holding the buck securely on his back. After making a hearty supper off the bear-meat, and dressing the wounds of the dogs,—which, by the way, healed rapidly, considering their terrible nature and the fact that I had nothing but bear's-grease to dress them with,—I hobbled "Coffee," and, being thoroughly exhausted, rolled myself up in a buffalo-robe, and was soon fast asleep: only to be awakened in a few hours by the nasty yelping of the wretched coyotes. Though there were probably less than a half-dozen of them, it sounded as though the whole canine race was present. I did not dare make a fire large enough to run them off. When I had finally come to the conclusion that the best thing I could do was to grin and bear it, the shrill cry of a mountain-lion aroused the dogs and also put to flight the coyotes, and I spent the remainder of the night in comparative peace and quietness.

Kentuck's cold nose coming in contact with my neck, in his efforts to share my robe, aroused me about daylight; and, not waiting for an extensive toilet and dainty breakfast, I broke camp and set out for home. Ten o'clock found me crossing Slate Creek, a few miles from the stockade. Looking down the creek, I saw a doe feeding at the mouth of a small gulch several hundred yards away, and quickly led "Coffee" and the dogs out of sight, with the intention of stalking her, forgetting at the moment the condition of my rifle. Just then I saw her start, look down the creek, toss her tail up, and dart into the bushes. Wondering what could have so startled her, I cautiously crept from out the coulée by which I was approaching her, and to my surprise saw, a couple of hundred yards still further down the creek, an Indian on foot. He crossed fearlessly, almost carelessly, and walked up on to a high point of ground jutting out into the valley or creek bottom he had just crossed. After a swift glance up and down the creek he turned, parted the bushes in front of him, and disappeared. I readily recognized him even at that distance as an Ogallala Sioux. After waiting probably ten minutes to assure myself there were no others with him, knowing it was seldom if ever they are seen alone on foot, I proceeded down the creek, intending to learn if he was heading in the direction of the stockade.

When just at the identical spot where I had last seen the Indian, an unearthly screech sounded in the chaparral a few feet in front of me, followed instantly by the bang of a gun, and I felt a blow on my side which nearly turned me around. What thoughts chased themselves through my excited imagination as I felt that terrible bullet plowing its way through my vitals will never be told. Then, as visions of the whole Sioux tribe dancing around my scalpless body vanished, I realized the truth. A disturbed sand-hill crane, that had alighted there during my detour, had screeched almost in my ear, and my stockless rifle, which I was carrying at full cock, had been discharged, nearly fracturing my ribs by the recoil. I felt truly thankful that California Joe was not present, for if my hair did not actually stand on end, I certainly had all the sensations of this once experienced never to be forgotten feeling.

With a sigh of relief I went back to "Coffee" and the dogs, and after cinching up the former until he looked like a wasp, and arranging the compress on Kentuck, I struck out for French Creek at a trot that hustled both the crippled dogs and overloaded "Coffee" to keep up with. Upon coming down into French Creek valley, about two miles above the stockade, another and greater surprise awaited me; for there I found encamped a party of prospectors, arrived from Fort Fetterman. As I had not for months set eyes upon any white man except my own immediate party, this was a treat as pleasant as it was unexpected. The fact that "Coffee" boldly deserted me here did not deter me from staying to dinner, especially when I saw they had both coffee and flapjacks,—delicacies that I had not reveled in for some weeks past. After spending an hour with them, I started down the creek, leaving poor Kentuck thoroughly exhausted from loss of blood, and unable to walk another step. To the astonishment of the boys, I walked into the stockade with a piece of bacon swinging in one hand and a sack of flour on my back. I doubt if they would have been more surprised had I walked in with General Grant and Queen Victoria on either arm.

"Coffee" had made a bee-line for home, anxious to be relieved of a load he had carried continuously for almost twenty-four hours. As I was so long in following him, they were beginning to feel alarmed at the continued absence of "Blue Grass,"—a name given me by Joe, and one that clung to me throughout my stay in the Black Hills.

That night we went up to the new camp and sat around a blazing log-heap, listening to the news from "the States" until long after midnight. Kentuck we swung in a blanket, taking turn about carrying him home, and it was many weeks before he was again in condition to accompany me on a hunt.

Roger D. Williams.

Big Game in the Rockies

Some eight or ten years ago it was by no means difficult, for one who knew where to go and how to hunt, to get excellent shooting in northwestern Wyoming. Large game was then moderately abundant, with the exception of buffalo. The latter had just been exterminated, but, bleaching in the sun, the ghastly evidences of man's sordid and selfish policy lay exposed at every step.

Indian troubles of a very formidable character did a great deal toward keeping the game intact in this portion of the country by keeping the white man out, and while other parts of Wyoming grew, and towns sprang up with rapid growth to become in an incredibly short time cities, involving in destruction, as the past sad history shows, the wild animals in their vicinity, this Northwestern portion remained unsettled, and acted as an asylum to receive within its rocky mountain-ranges and vast sheltering forests the scattering bands of elk and deer fleeing from annihilation and the encroaching haunts of men. As soon as it was safe then, and in some instances unquestionably before, cattlemen, not inaptly styled pioneers of civilization, began to drift down along the valley of the Big Horn, and, like the patriarchs of old, "brought their flocks with them," settling here and there, wherever they could find advantageous sites for their ranches.

On the Heights.
From Scribner's Magazine.

And now, as I propose to give some hunting experiences of those days, if you will accompany me to Billings, on the Northern Pacific Railway, the nearest town to my ranch and the Mecca to which the devout cattleman drives his wagon for supplies, I will introduce you to the foot-hills and mountains, and some of the adventures therein.

After four days on a sleeping-car, it is a delightful release to tumble out on a frosty September morning, and, being guided to where the ranch-wagon and crew are bivouacked just outside the limits of the rapidly growing town, to get one's breakfast on terra firma. No time is now to be wasted; the mules are hitched up; the little band of horses are rounded together, and when we have jumped into our saddles, the cook, who always handles the reins, gives a crack of his whip, and we take our departure from civilization. A couple of miles brings us to a primitive wire-rope ferry, where we cross the Yellowstone River, which at this season of the year is low and clear; in a few minutes we are over, and, ascending the bluffs on the other side, take our last look at the beautiful valley we are leaving behind.

By night we reach Pryor's Creek, and picking out as good a camping-place as possible, the mules are soon unhitched and with the horses turned loose to graze. While the cook is preparing the evening meal, I bag a few prairie-chickens to give variety to the fare. Breakfasting at daylight the next morning, we are soon under way again, with Pryor's Mountains in the distance as our goal for this day's journey. Toward evening the white tepees of an Indian camp are visible clustered in a picturesque group close to Pryor's Mountains. Passing them, not without paying a slight tribute in the way of tobacco and such other gifts as our copper-colored friends generally demand, we fairly enter Pryor's Gap, and there, in a beautiful amphitheater, we again make camp. This evening we must have trout for supper, so all hands go to work, and we are soon rewarded with a fine mess of trout from the head waters of Pryor's Creek.

The next day, as we reach the summit of the gap, one of the most beautiful views in the country opens out. The great main range of the Rocky Mountains stretches before us, its rugged, snow-capped peaks glistening in the morning sun, and we long to be there, but many a long mile still intervenes, and forty-four miles of desert has to be crossed today. This is always an arduous undertaking. It is monotonous in the extreme, and men and animals are sure to suffer for want of good water, for after leaving Sage Creek on the other side of the gap, there is no water to be had until Stinking Water River[A] is reached. But all things must have an end, and at last, late in the evening, we find ourselves encamped on the banks of that stream, beautiful despite its unfortunate name.

[A] Bancroft, in his account of the early explorations of Wyoming, refers to this river as follows: "It is a slander to use this non-descriptive name for an inoffensive stream. The early trappers took it from the Indians, who, in their peculiar fashion, called it 'the river that ran by the stinking water,' referring to bad-smelling hot springs on its banks."

Fording the river the next morning, not a very terrifying operation in its present low stage, we climb the steep bank and soon begin our long ascent of the divide that separates us from our ranch and Greybull River. Accompanied by an immense amount of expletives, and very bad language, the mules are finally induced to gain the summit. Here even the most casual observer could not fail to be impressed with the magnificent and apparently indefinite expanse of mountain scenery, that, turn which way he will, meets his view. However, we have no time to linger, and picking our way among the countless buffalo wallows which indent the level surface of the summit, the wagon, with its wheels double locked, is soon groaning and creaking down the descent, which leads to the merrily rushing Meeteetse, following which, down to its junction with Greybull, we are soon inside our own fence, and are joyously welcomed by the dogs. Here, too, I find my trusty friend and companion of all my hunting trips, Tazwell Woody, a grizzled veteran of the mountains, who once long ago claimed Missouri as his home. From the ranch to the mountains is a comparatively short trip, for one day's travel to the westward would place you well up on their slopes.

Let me say of this portion of the range that it is the most rugged, broken, and precipitous of its whole extent, and the charm of overcoming its apparent inaccessibility can only be appreciated by one who has toiled and sweated in surmounting the difficulties of mountain travel from a pure love of nature in its wildest and grandest form.

Experience having taught me long ago that it was well nigh impossible to get good specimens of all the different varieties of big game on any one trip, I made up my mind to devote a certain amount of time each year to one variety. By this means their habits could be studied more closely, and the main point never lost sight of. In a short paper like this I may best take up the chief of these varieties one by one, and, without regard to the time of their occurrence, tell something of my experiences with each. And first, as to perhaps the shyest, the Rocky Mountain sheep.

In the pursuit of Rocky Mountain sheep, the hunter, to be successful, must have a fondness for the mountains, a sure foot, good wind, and a head which no height will turn. These requisites, with patience and perseverance, will, sooner or later, as the hunter gains experience, reward him with ample returns. Sometimes, however, the unexpected will happen, and the following tale may serve as an example.

We were camping well up in the mountains, and almost any hour of the day sheep could be seen with the glasses. I was after sheep; it was my intent, business, and purpose to get some if possible, and all my energies were concentrated in that direction.

There were two fine rams in particular that we could see about a mile and a half from camp occupying the slope of a rocky point or promontory that jutted out from a spur of the range. These two had a commanding position, for, while it seemed impossible to get to them from above, they could see every movement from below or on each side of them. However, after studying the country for two days, I found that by ascending the mountain behind them and coming down again I could still keep above them, though there was a very narrow ledge of rocks, rather a hazardous place, that had to be crossed to get to the point they were on. This narrow ledge they had to come back on to get to the main part of the mountain; so, stationing my companion there, and taking off my shoes, and putting on an extra pair of heavy stockings, I proceeded to crawl toward the sheep.

With due care, and not making a sound, I made a most successful stalk. Peering over the ledge, I raised my head just enough to be sure my game was still there. They were there, sure enough, within seventy-five yards of me, totally unconscious of danger, when all of a sudden they sprang to their feet and dashed away from below me as though possessed of a devil. I fired hastily, but of course missed, and turning, tried to run back to head them off, wondering what had started them, as I knew I had made no noise. But running over broken rock in one's stocking feet is a very different thing from the slow, deliberate movements that brought me there, and besides, in a few seconds I had the mortification of seeing my would-be victims bounding across the narrow ledge that separated them from the mountain. However, I thought with satisfaction that at least one would meet its death from my companion in hiding; but, alas! although the rams almost knocked him down, his cartridge missed fire, and the game ran safely by.

Regaining my shoes, which was a great relief, I soon joined my companion, and then discovered the curious adventure I had been made the subject of. It seems that when I had reached a point well down on the promontory I must have disturbed a cougar, which was evidently there for the same purpose I was, and which had stealthily followed me as I proceeded toward the sheep. Old Woody described it as highly amusing—I sneaking down after the rams, and the panther sneaking down upon me. As soon as the beast got an opportunity, it turned off, and, making the descent, alarmed the rams and thus made my hunt a failure.

**Stalking the Stalker.
From Scribner's Magazine.**

For several days I watched this point, but those rams never came back to it again. However, not long after this I was amply rewarded, and secured a fine specimen. From one of the high ledges I was looking down into a sort of amphitheater shut in by massive rocky heights. In this secluded retreat a little band of ewes, with one grand old patriarch as their master, could be seen every day disporting themselves with many a curious gambol. After many unsuccessful attempts, I was enabled to get a shot, and great was my delight at depriving the little band of their supercilious protector. Upon another occasion I was camping away back up in the mountains, where there were about eighteen inches of snow on the ground. The weather had been villainous; there was no meat in the camp, and I determined to see if I could not get a deer. The prospect was not very cheering, for shortly after starting a heavy fog shut down, hiding all objects from view. I had not proceeded far, however, when I struck the fresh track of a ram, and, following it cautiously for about a mile through the open, it led into a dense patch of pine on the side of the mountain. Proceeding very carefully now, I soon made out the outline of a fine old ram that had wandered off here in the timber to be by himself. Giving him no time to run, for I was close upon him, certainly not farther than twenty-five yards, I planted a shot just back of the shoulder, but he did not seem to mind it. I gave him another when he started to walk slowly off. One more shot in the same place, and down he came. Even then he died hard. Such is the vitality of an old ram; for upon examining him I found his heart all torn to pieces. This was a good head of nearly sixteen inches circumference of horns, and the girth of chest was forty-six inches. In returning to camp for horses to pack him on, I jumped five more sheep, but having done well enough, they were allowed to disappear in safety.

Sheep have a wonderfully keen vision, and it is absolutely useless to try to get to them if they once see you, unless you happen to be above them and on their favorite runway; then they huddle together and try to break back past you. The only safe rule is to travel high and keep working up above their feeding-grounds. In the spring of the year they are much easier to kill than in the fall, for then the heavy winter snows have driven them out of the mountains, and they come low down after the fresh green grass. The rams are then in bands, having laid aside the hostility that later in the year seems to possess each and every one of them.

I was much interested once in watching a band of eight rams, all of them old fellows. They would feed early in the morning and then betake themselves to a large rock which stood on a grassy slope, where they would play for hours. One of them would jump on the rock and challenge the others to butt him off. Two or three would then jump up, and their horns would come together with a clash that I could hear from my position, which was fully a quarter of a mile away. On one occasion I saw them suddenly stop their play and each ram became fixed; there the little band stood as though carved out of stone. They remained that way for quite half an hour without a movement. I could not detect with the glasses the slightest motion, when, presently, three strange rams made their appearance. Here was the explanation that I was looking for. They had seen them long before I had. The three visitors were not very well received, but were compelled to beat an ignominious and hasty retreat up the mountain side.

As summer draws near, and the winter snow begins to disappear, bands of elk may be seen migrating toward their favorite ranges. The bulls are now together in bands of greater or less extent. Their horns are well grown out, but are soft and in the velvet. The cows and calves stick closely to the thick timber. As the season advances and the flies become troublesome, the bulls will get up as high as they can climb and seem to delight in standing on the brink of some mountain precipice. I have often wondered, in seeing them standing thus, whether they were insensible of the magnificent scenery that surrounded them.

Reader, what would you have given to have seen, as I have, a band of two hundred and fifty bull-elk collected together on a beautiful piece of green grassy turf at an elevation of nine thousand feet? Here was a sight to make a man's nerves tingle. This was the largest band of bulls, by actual count, that I have ever seen, though my cousin and partner once saw in the fall of the year, including bulls, cows, and calves, fifteen hundred. This was on the memorable occasion when the only elk ever killed by any of my men gave up his life, and we have all concluded that this particular elk was frightened to death; for though three men shot at him and each was confident he hit him, they always asserted afterward that no bullet-mark could be found on him.

Generally, in August, in each band of bulls there will be found one or two barren cows. About the end of August, after the bulls have rubbed the velvet off their antlers, they will come back to the vicinity of the bands of cows. I have seen bulls as late as September 4 peaceably feeding or resting among the bands of cows. Usually, in a band of fifty cows, there would be three or four males, including, possibly, one or two spike-bulls.[A] I have seen these spike-bulls in the velvet as late as September 4, though by that time the older bulls had mostly rubbed the velvet off. A little later, about September 7, the bulls begin to challenge each other,—in hunting parlance, "to whistle." This, on a clear, frosty night, is sometimes extremely melodious, and it is one of the most impossible sounds to imitate. Hunting elk, if I may be pardoned for saying it, I do not consider very exciting sport to a man thoroughly versed in the woods. They are far too noble an animal to kill unnecessarily, and if one hunts them in September, when they are whistling, it is a very easy matter, guided by the sound, to stalk them successfully.

[A] A spike-bull is a young elk carrying his first or dag antlers. These are single-tined, though in rare instances they are bifurcated.

Studying the Strangers.
From Scribner's Magazine.

Elk, like the rest of the deer family, are excessively fond of saline matter. Their trails may be seen leading from every direction to the great alkaline licks that abound in certain parts of their mountain-ranges. Among other favorite resorts are springs, which make, on steep wooded slopes, delightful, boggy wallowing places. The bulls revel in these from August to the middle of September. It is not an uncommon thing to kill them just as they emerge from their viscous bath coated with mud. The elk has a great deal of natural curiosity, and I have seen extraordinary instances of this where they had been but little hunted or alarmed. My friend Phillips, of Washington, who was with me, will vouch for the veracity of this story, which I give as an example: We were wandering along the top of the mountain, some nine thousand feet up, trying to stalk some elk, not to shoot them, but to photograph them. We jumped a small band of bulls, numbering about sixteen. They trotted off slowly, frequently stopping to look back, until all but two large bulls had disappeared. These walked slowly back to within fifty yards of where we were standing, and stopped, facing us.

It was truly one of the most charming sights one could have wished for, to have those graceful, sleek creatures almost close enough to caress. Presently, with a defiant snort, and with a succession of short barks, they would move away and come back again, repeating these manœuvers over and over again, until we got tired of trying to look like a brace of marble posts and sat down. We thought this would frighten them, but it did not, and once I thought they were going to proceed from curiosity to more offensive operations, so close did they come to us. Even my caterwauling, as my friend unfeelingly characterized my attempt to imitate their challenges, did not seem to alarm them, and not until a full half-hour had elapsed did this pair of inquisitive worthies at length jog off.

Elk are vigorous fighters, and while it seems that their combats seldom terminate fatally, the broken points of their antlers, and their scarred and bruised bodies, bear testimony to the severity of their encounters. A full-grown elk stands about sixteen hands high, is about eight feet two inches long from nose to tip of tail, and with a girth around the chest of about six feet.

It was on the head of Wind River that I secured my largest head. The regularity of the points was somewhat marred, as the bull had evidently been fighting only a short time before I killed him. These horns were not very massive, but the length, measured along the outside curve, is sixty-three and seven eighths inches. The circumference between bay and tray is from seven and one half to eight inches, and the greatest spread between antlers is forty-nine inches.

Probably more horrible lies have been told by bear-hunters than any other class of men, except, perhaps, fishermen, who are renowned for their yarns. However, I trust that in the case of the few instances I have to give of my experience I can keep fairly within the bounds of truth and not try the reader's credulity.

Bear-hunting, as a general rule, I do not think would appeal to most sportsmen. It is rather slow work, and one is often very inadequately rewarded for the amount of time and trouble spent in hunting up Bruin. There is hardly a portion of the mountains where there are not evidences of bears, but I do not believe that in any locality they are especially abundant. They have been hunted and trapped so long that those which survive are extremely cautious. In my experience there is no animal gifted with a greater amount of intelligence, and, in this region, the hunter's chief virtue, patience to wait and stay in one spot, is sure to be rewarded, sooner or later, with a good shot which should mean success.

Let me say that the danger and ferocity of the bear is, I think, very much over-stated, yet there is just enough of the element of danger to make the pursuit of this animal exciting. Naturalists do not now apparently recognize more than two varieties of bear in the Rocky Mountains; that is, they class the cinnamon, silver-tip, and grizzly as grizzly bear. The other variety, of course, is the black bear. I am by no means sure that the grizzly bear will not be further subdivided after careful comparisons of collections of skulls.

Much has been said and written about the size and weight of the grizzly bear, and in most instances this has been mere guesswork. Lewis and Clark made frequent mention of this animal, and yet their estimates of the weight fall far below that of other writers. Only a few instances have come to my knowledge where the weight has been ascertained absolutely. A good-sized grizzly killed in Yellowstone Park one summer by Wilson, the Government scout, weighed six hundred pounds. Colonel Pickett, who has a neighboring ranch to mine, and who has killed more bears than any man I know of, weighed his largest, which, if I remember rightly, weighed eight hundred pounds. One will, of course, occasionally see a very large skin, and from its size it would seem impossible that the animal that once filled it out, if in good condition, could have weighed less than twelve hundred pounds. But I think it may be safely set down that the average weight of most specimens that one will get in the mountains will be under, rather than over, five hundred pounds.

To me, bear-hunting possesses a great fascination, and for years I have hunted nothing else. Personally I prefer to go after them in the spring. Their skins are then in their prime, the hair long and soft, and their claws (if valued as they should be) are long and sharp from disuse. Bears seek their winter quarters in Bad Lands and in the mountains. Those that adopt the former come out much earlier; consequently if the hunter is on the ground soon enough, by beginning first in the lower lands and working toward the mountains, he may be reasonably sure of securing good skins as late as June. In the spring, too, bears are much more in the open, and travel incessantly in search of food.

It is highly interesting to watch them, when one has the chance, turning over stones, tearing open fallen trees, or rooting like a pig in some favorite spot. Acres upon acres even of hard, stony ground they will turn up, and in other places it would be difficult to find a stone or rock they had not displaced. They will undermine and dig out great stumps. Ant-hills you will find leveled, and the thrifty squirrels, who have labored all the previous fall to make a cache of pine nuts, are robbed on sight.

One spring, the work on the ranch being done, Woody and I took our pack-horses and proceeded to the mountains after bears. I had no sooner picked out a good camping-ground than it began to snow, and for four days we could not stir from camp. However, it finally cleared off, the sun came out bright and warm, and the little stream that we were on began boiling, tearing, and rushing along, full to the banks, causing us to move our camp back to higher ground. After breakfast, as we proposed to take a long day's trip, we took our horses with us. Riding up to the head of the stream we were on, looking for bears, no signs were to be seen, though plenty of sheep were in sight all the time. Riding on, away above the cañon some six or eight miles we could see some elk. We closely scanned the neighboring heights, but still no sign of bears. Finally, we turned off and worked our way clear up on top of the mountain, determined to see the country anyway. Slowly we climbed upward, skyward, dragging our weary horses after us, until at noon we were nearly up and concluded to lunch at the little rill of melted snow that came from a big drift on the mountain-side.

To get to it, though, we were obliged to cross the drift, and Woody led the way with his favorite horse, old Rock, in tow; and here was where my laugh came in, to see those two floundering through that drift. At times, all I could see of Rock was the tips of his ears. The crust was just strong enough to hold Woody up if he went "easy," but he could not go easy with the horse plunging on top of him, and they would both break through. However, they had to go ahead in spite of themselves, and they were finally landed half-drowned and smothered on dry ground. Of course, profiting by this experience, I circumnavigated the drift, and we sat down to our dry bread and bacon, washed down by a long pull from the handy snow-water. Ten minutes and a pipe was all that we allowed ourselves before resuming our toil—for that is really the way to designate the ascent of these mountains.

We saw six fine rams which did not seem to regard us with any uneasiness, permitting us to get within murderous distance, and I looked at their leader with some longing. He had such a noble head of curling, graceful, well-rounded horns. He must have been a powerful adversary when it came to butting. Stifling the desire, I passed by without disturbing them, and at last reached the top of the divide, and was repaid by a glorious and most extended view.

At that time Nature was not in her most smiling garb. It had been steadily growing colder, ominous clouds were gathering in the west, and an ugly rolling of thunder warned us that no genial spring day with shirt-sleeve accompaniment was to gladden and cheer us. Still we must look for bears; so buttoning up our coats and turning up our collars we surveyed the country. At the same time it was impossible to forego a study of the grandeur of the view displayed before us.

Those who have seen the mountains and foot-hills only in the fall of the year, when every blade of grass is parched and brown and dry, can form no adequate idea of the change that presents itself in the spring. Especially is one surprised when, standing on the top of some mountain height surrounded by everlasting snow, he looks down over the valleys and sees the richness and vividness of the green growing grasses which seem to roll up almost to his feet. As we stood there we had a glorious panorama. The vast gathering cloud was behind us, and the sun, though not shining for us, was lighting up the broad valley below. Greybull River stretched away until it joined the Big Horn beyond. The whole range of the Big Horn Mountains was visible, their snow-tops glistening like a bank of silver clouds, and the main range we were standing on was brought out in all its dazzling grandeur. Snow-drift upon snow-drift, with gracefully curling crests, stretched away as far as the eye could reach, for miles and miles. Still we saw no bears, and while we were enjoying all this wonderful scenery we neglected the storm, and were soon enveloped in a raging tempest of wind and snow with a demoniacal accompaniment of lightning and crashing thunder.

We hunched up our backs and stumbled along the ridge before the blast, and were soon brought up by a drift. However, here was luck for once. We saw the print of two fresh bear-tracks crossing the drift. All thoughts of the storm were lost in our delight at the vicinity of bears, for the sign was very fresh. Alas, though, we lost the tracks after crossing the drift, and could not find them again upon the rugged soil of these ridges where the wind had blown the snow off. We circled round and round, studying every patch of snow, and my companion, Woody, looked and spoke doubtfully. At last I caught the trail again. Only a half-dozen tracks, but enough to show the right direction, and as we ascended the ridge the tracks were on, I saw the two rascals across the gulch on an enormous snow-drift, tearing and chewing at something, I could not make out what.

**Crossing a Drift.
From Scribner's Magazine.**

It was still snowing hard, but it was only a squall and nearly over. The wind was wrong; it unfortunately blew toward the bears and the only direction in which we could stalk them. Still an attempt had to be made. We took the bridles from our horses and let down our hacamores, to let them feed comfortably and out of sight, while we crawled up the ridge to where it joined the one the bears were on. We had to creep up a beastly snow-drift, which was soft and no telling how deep.

It was deep enough, for we went through sometimes to our armpits. But what mattered it when we were at concert-pitch, and bears for the tune? We were now on the same ridge as the bears. Cautiously, with the wind just a little aslant, we crawled down toward our prey, crossing another miserable snow-drift, into which we went up to our necks, where we brought up, our feet having touched bottom. We floundered out behind a small rock, and then looked up over at the bears. Too far to shoot with any certainty, and I said to Woody, "I must get closer." And so back we crawled.

Making a little detour we bobbed up again, not serenely, for the wind was blowing on the backs of our necks straight as an arrow to where the bears were. But we were a little higher up on the ridge than they and our taint must have gone over them, for when I looked up again one of them was chewing a savory morsel, and the other was on his hind legs blinking at the sun, which was just breaking through the clouds. Wiping the snow and drops of water and slush from our rifles and sights, and with a whispered advice from Woody not to be in a hurry if they came toward us, but to reserve fire in order to make sure work,—for no sheltering tree awaited us as a safe retreat, nothing but snowy ridges for miles,—I opened the ball with the young lady who was sitting down.

Two Pairs.
From Scribner's Magazine.

She dropped her bone, clapped one of her paws to her ribs, and to my happiness waltzed down the snow-bank. As she now seemed to be out of the dance, I turned to her brother, for such I afterward judged him to be, who, with great affection, had gone down with her until she stuck her head in the snow. Not understanding this, he smelled around his fallen relative, when a hollow three-hundred-and-thirty-grain chunk of lead nearly severed one hip and smashed the other. He did not stop to reason, but promptly jumped on his relative, and then and there occurred a lively bit of a scrimmage. Over and over they rolled, slapping, biting, and making the best fight of it they could, considering the plight they were in. Each probably accused the other of the mishap.

The snow was dyed a crimson hue. It was like the scene of a bloody battle-ground. At last the lady first aggrieved gave up, and plunged her head back into the snow, while her brother, not having any one to fight with, went off a short distance and lay down. We cautiously approached, bearing in mind that a snow-drift is a hard thing for pedestrians in a hurry to travel on, and when we got about ten feet from the first bear, I told my companion to snowball her and see what effect that would have, for she looked too innocent to be finished for and dead.

But instead of doing so, he discarded his rifle and reached for her tail. Ah, I thought so! for, as he gave a yank, up came her head, her jaws flew open like clockwork, and a snort came forth. But right between the eyes went the deadly messenger, smashing her skull and ending any prolonged suffering for any of us. Her end accomplished, we turned to the other partner. He had been taking it all in, and was ready for a fight. He seemed pretty fit, too. Fortunately, he could not come up to us; the snow-drift was too steep, and he had only two serviceable legs to travel with. Still he had true grit, and faced us; but it was an unequal battle.

Again the bullet reached its victim, and brother ba'r lay quietly on his back with his legs in the air. No need to trifle with this bear's tail, as any fool could see that he was dead. However, we pelted him with a lot of snowballs, and then Woody went around to his stump of a tail and pulled it while I stood guard at his head. We took off our coats, and soon had the skins off the pair of them. These skins proved to be in the finest condition, though the bears themselves were poor. I should judge one was a three-year-old and the other a two-year-old. Still they were good-sized grizzlies.

Those skins seemed to grow in size and weight as each of us lugged one up the side of the mountain over shelving rock, snow, and loose gravel to where we left our horses. Of course they were not there, and we had to go on, carrying the skins, which were growing heavier and heavier every minute, until we tracked our horses to where they were feeding, and, in Western vernacular, "we had a circus" packing those skins on my horse. It was done at last, though, and to stay, by means of blindfolding him with a coat; and after a little while he settled down to work as though he had carried bears all his many years of service. I had a very nasty time in getting down the mountain after my horse slipped and fell down a gap in the crown rock. We could not get the other down, so I took charge of my horse and skins and made the rest of the descent in safety, though it looked squally for a bit when the old rascal's feet slid out from under him, knocking me down in the snow, and he on top, and I could feel that even with the fleecy covering the rocks were still very hard.

However, it was deep enough for me to crawl out, more scared than hurt, and soon we had sage-brush and grass under our feet, with an easy trail to camp, where a square meal inside of a stomach that sorely needed it soon made amends for all hardships. Wondering what those bears had been at work at, I went back the next day and found that they had been tearing up a sheep that had died of scab, a disease that wild sheep are subject to.

To a thorough sportsman, killing bear after a successful stalk is by long odds the best and most exciting method, but the country must be such as permits of this,—as, for instance, when there are long stretches of high mountains, plateaus or ridges above, or devoid of, timber, where the bears resort to root, and where the hunter from some elevated post can look over a large area with the aid of glasses. The general procedure, though, is to put out bait—that is, to have the carcass of some animal to attract the bear, and many a noble elk or timorous deer has been thus sacrificed. To avoid this needless destruction it has been my custom to take along on my hunting-trips aged and worn-out horses, which answer admirably when it comes to drawing bears to a carcass.

Of course, this is not always a sure way, for the bear, if alarmed or disturbed, will only visit the carcass at night, and then, if the hunter is persistent and determined to get a shot, he may expect many weary hours of watching from a friendly pine.

I think I hear the reader say, "What's the fun in shooting a bear from a tree?—there is no risk in that." True, there is not; but it is when you come down from your perch that you may not feel quite so safe, as with limbs benumbed from cold and lack of circulation you climb down, knowing that perhaps several pairs of watchful eyes or cunning nostrils are studying your movements. Involuntarily your thoughts travel in the vein of your gloomy surroundings as you go stumbling on your way to camp: what if the bear should prefer live goose-flesh to dead horse?

One spring morning I was knocking around under the base of the mountains and found myself, about dinner-time, so close to Colonel Pickett's cozy log-cabin that I determined to pay him a long-postponed visit. After an ample repast, including some delicious home-made butter, which I had not tasted for a month, Woody and I, with our little pack-train, regretfully filed off, and, fording the river, took up our wanderings, not expecting to see our cheery host again for a year.

We had not proceeded far, though, when we met an excited "cow-puncher," who evidently had news to tell. He had been up on the side of the mountain, which was here a long grassy slope as smooth as any of our well-tended lawns, extending upward to where it joined the dense pine-forest which covered the upper portion of the mountain. Our friend was the horse-wrangler for a neighboring ranch, and was out looking for horses. Did any one ever see a horse-wrangler who was not looking for missing stock?

When skirting the timber he surprised, or was surprised by, a good-sized grizzly, which promptly chased him downward and homeward, and evidently for a short distance was well up in the race. Gathering from his description that the bear had been at work on the carcass of a steer that had died from eating poison-weed, I determined to go back and camp, and see if another skin could not be added to the score. It did not take long to pick out an ideal camping-spot, well sheltered, with plenty of dry wood, and trout from the little stream almost jumping into the frying-pan.

Our horses had been having pretty rough times lately, and they lost no time in storing away as much of the rich grass as they could hold. They had plenty of society, too, for the slope was dotted here and there with bunches of range cattle and bands of horses, not to mention the recent additions to the families of each in the shape of frolicsome calves and frisky foals, all busily at work. Bruin seemed rather out of place in such a pastoral scene, and yet, as one looked higher beyond the somber heights of the forest toward the frowning crown rock that resembled some mighty fortress forbidding further progress, or the everlasting snow-peaks above, one could well fancy that wild animals must be up there somewhere, either in the dense woods or in the still higher and safer retreats.

We at once examined the ground, and found the carcasses of two steers, one of which was untouched, but the other was very nearly devoured. All the signs pointed to more than one bear, and the ground was fairly padded down round the carcass they were using. Unfortunately, though, there seemed to be no place to watch from,— not a bush or rock to screen one while awaiting a shot. To cut a long story short, I watched that bait every afternoon and evening for a week, and though it was visited every night I never got a sight of the prowlers. Bears will very often, when going to a carcass, take the same trail, but when leaving, wander off in almost any direction. Taking advantage of this, and being satisfied that they were up in the timber through the day, we hunted for their trail, and found it on an old wood-road that led through the timber. To make sure, we placed the hind quarters of one of the steers just on the edge of the forest, and awaited developments. That night the bears found it, and, dragging it off, carefully cached it; so we determined to watch here.

As the daylight faded that night I was much disappointed to find that if I was to get a shot it would have to be in the dark; so as soon as I found I could not see to shoot with any degree of safety, I got up in a pine-tree that commanded the road and was just over the bait. It was weary work watching, and to make it still more uncomfortable, a heavy thunder-storm swept by, first pelting one with hail, then with a deluge of rain and snow.

It was pitch-dark, except when the black recesses of the forest seemed to be rent asunder during the vivid lightning. The whole effect was weird and uncanny, and I wished myself back under my soft, warm blankets. I could not well repress thinking of the early admonition of "Never go under a tree during a thunder-storm."—But what's that? One swift surge of blood to the heart, an involuntary tightening of the muscles that strongly gripped the rifle. I seemed to feel, rather than see, the presence of three strange objects that appeared to have sprung from the ground under me.

I had not heard a sound; not a twig had snapped, and yet, as I strained my eyes to penetrate the gloom, there, right at my feet, almost touching them in fact, I made out the indistinct forms of three bears all standing on their hind legs. Oh, what a chance it was if it had not been so dark! I could not even see the end of my rifle; but I knew I could hit them, they were so close. But to hit fatally? Well, there is no use thinking about it now the bears are here. Trust to luck and shoot!

Hardly daring to breathe, I fired; the scuffling on the ground, and the short, sharp snorting, told me I had not missed; but I could see nothing, and could only hear the bear rolling over and over and growling angrily. Presently there was quiet, and then with angry, furious champing of jaws the wounded animal charged back directly under me; but I could not see to shoot again, worse luck. From sundry sounds I gathered the bear was not far off, but had lain down in a thicket which was about one hundred yards from my tree. I could hear an occasional growl, and the snap of dead branches, broken as she turned uneasily. I did not know exactly what to do. To descend was awkward, and to stay where I was, wet and chilled to the bone, seemed impossible. It was most unlikely the other bears would come back; however, thinking it would be prudent to stay aloft a little while longer, I made up my mind to stick it out another half hour. During this wait I fancied I could see shadowy forms moving about, and I could surely hear a cub squalling. The light was now a little better, and the darkness, though still very black, was not so intense.

Just as I had screwed up courage to descend, another bear came up under the tree and reared up. This time I made no mistake, and almost simultaneously with the rifle's report a hoarse bawl proved to me that I had conquered. Glad at almost any cost to get out of my cramped position I sung out to Woody to lend a hand, as I proposed descending, and as he came up I came down, and then we discussed the situation. The proximity of the wounded bear was not pleasant, but then the dead one must be opened in order to save the skin. But what if the latter were not dead? Hang this night-work! why can't the bears stick to daylight! But to work,—there was the motionless form to be operated on. Inch by inch we crept up with our rifles at full-cock stuck out ahead of us until they gently touched the inanimate mass. It was all right, for the bear was stone-dead. Hastily feeling in the dark, as neatly as possible the necessary operations were nearly concluded when simultaneously we both dropped our knives and made for the open.... It makes me perspire even now when I think of that midnight stampede from an enraged and wounded grizzly.

Archibald Rogers.

Coursing the Prongbuck

The prongbuck is the most characteristic and distinctive of American game animals. Zoölogically speaking, its position is unique. It is the only hollow-horned ruminant which sheds its horns. We speak of it as an antelope, and it does of course represent on our prairies the antelopes of the Old World, and is a distant relative of theirs; but it stands apart from all other horned animals. Its position in the natural world is almost as lonely as that of the giraffe.

The chase of the prongbuck has always been to me very attractive, but especially so when carried on by coursing it with greyhounds. Any man who has lived much in the cow-country, and has wandered about a good deal over the great plains, is of course familiar with this gallant little beast, and has probably had to rely upon it very frequently for a supply of fresh meat. On my ranch it has always been the animal which yielded us most of the fresh meat we had in the spring and summer. Of course at such times we killed only bucks, and even these only when we positively needed the flesh.

In all its ways and habits the prongbuck differs as much from deer and elk as from goat and sheep. Now that the buffalo has gone, it is the only game really at home on the wide plains. It is a striking-looking little creature, with its big bulging eyes, single-pronged horns, and the sharply contrasted coloration of its coat; this coat, by the way, being composed of curiously coarse and brittle hair. In marked contrast to deer, antelope never seek to elude observation; all they care for is to be able to see themselves. As they have good noses and wonderful eyes, and as they live by preference where there is little or no cover, shots at them are usually obtained only at far longer range than is the case with other game; and yet, as they are easily seen, and often stand looking at the hunter just barely within very long rifle-range, they are always tempting their pursuer to the expenditure of cartridges. More shots are wasted at antelope than at any other game. They would be even harder to secure were it not that they are subject to fits of panic, folly, or excessive curiosity, which occasionally put them fairly at the mercy of the rifle-bearing hunter.

Prongbucks are very fast runners indeed, even faster than deer. They vary greatly in speed, however, precisely as is the case with deer; in fact, I think that the average hunter makes altogether too little account of this individual variation among different animals of the same kind. Under the same conditions different deer and antelope vary in speed and wariness, exactly as bears and cougars vary in cunning and ferocity.

When in perfect condition a full-grown buck antelope, from its strength and size, is faster and more enduring than an old doe; but a fat buck, before the rut has begun, will often be pulled down by a couple of good greyhounds much more speedily than a flying yearling or two-year-old doe. Under favorable circumstances, when the antelope was jumped near by, I have seen one overhauled and seized by a single first-class greyhound; and, on the other hand, I have more than once seen a pronghorn run away from a whole pack of just as good dogs. With a fair start, and on good ground, a thoroughbred horse, even though handicapped by the weight of a rider, will run down an antelope; but this is a feat which should rarely be attempted, because such a race, even when carried to a successful issue, is productive of the utmost distress to the steed.

Ordinary horses will sometimes run down an antelope which is slower than the average. I had on my ranch an under-sized old Indian pony named White Eye, which, when it was fairly roused, showed a remarkable turn of speed, and had great endurance. One morning on the round-up, when for some reason we did not work the cattle, I actually ran down an antelope in fair chase on this old pony. It was a nursing doe, and I came over the crest of a hill, between forty and fifty yards away from it. As it wheeled to start back, the old cayuse pricked up his ears with great interest, and the minute I gave him a sign was after it like a shot. Whether, being a cow-pony, he started to run it just as if it were a calf or a yearling trying to break out of the herd, or whether he was overcome by dim reminiscences of buffalo-hunting in his Indian youth, I know not. At any rate, after the doe he went, and in a minute or two I found I was drawing up to it. I had a revolver, but of course did not wish to kill her, and so got my rope ready to try to take her alive. She ran frantically, but the old pony, bending level to the ground, kept up his racing lope and closed right in beside her. As I came up she fairly bleated. An expert with the rope would have captured her with the utmost ease; but I missed, sending the coil across her shoulders. She again gave an agonized bleat, or bark, and wheeled around like a shot. The cow-pony stopped almost, but not quite, as fast, and she got a slight start, and it was some little time before I overhauled her again. When I did I repeated the performance, and this time when she wheeled she succeeded in getting on some ground where I could not follow, and I was thrown out.

I have done a good deal of coursing with greyhounds at one time or another, but always with scratch packs. The average frontiersman seems to have an inveterate and rooted objection to a dog with pure blood. If he gets a greyhound, his first thought is to cross it with something else, whether a bull mastiff, or a setter, or a foxhound. There are a few men who keep leashes of greyhounds of pure blood, bred and trained to antelope-coursing, and who do their coursing scientifically, carrying the dogs out to the hunting-grounds in wagons and exercising every care in the sport; but these men are rare. The average man who dwells where antelope are sufficiently abundant to make coursing a success, simply follows the pursuit at odd moments, with whatever long-legged dogs he and his neighbors happen to have; and his methods of coursing are apt to be as rough as his outfit. My own coursing has been precisely of this character. At different times I have had on my ranch one or two high-class greyhounds and Scotch deer-hounds, with which we have coursed deer and antelope, as well as jack-rabbits, foxes, and coyotes; and we have usually had with them one or two ordinary hounds, and various half-bred dogs. I must add, however, that some of the latter were very good. I can recall in particular one fawn-colored beast, a cross between a greyhound and a foxhound, which ran nearly as fast as the former, though it occasionally yelped in shrill tones. It could also trail well, and was thoroughly game; on one occasion it ran down and killed a coyote single-handed.

On going out with these dogs, I rarely chose a day when I was actually in need of fresh meat. If this was the case, I usually went alone with the rifle; but if one or two other men were at the ranch, and we wanted a morning's fun, we would often summon the dogs, mount our horses, and go trooping out to the antelope-ground. As there was a good deer-country between the ranch bottom and the plains where we found the prongbuck, it not infrequently happened that we had a chase after black-tail or white-tail on the way. Moreover, when we got out to the ground, before sighting antelope, it frequently happened that the dogs would jump a jack-rabbit or a fox, and away the whole set would go after it, streaking through the short grass, sometimes catching their prey in a few hundred yards, and sometimes having to run a mile or so. In consequence, by the time we reached the regular hunting-ground, the dogs were apt to have lost a good deal of their freshness. We would get them in behind the horses and creep cautiously along, trying to find some solitary prongbuck in a suitable place, where we could bring up the dogs from behind a hillock, and give them a fair start after it. Usually we failed to get the dogs near enough for a good start; and in most cases their chases after unwounded prongbuck resulted in the quarry running clean away from them. Thus the odds were greatly against them; but, on the other hand, we helped them wherever possible with the rifle. We often rode well scattered out, and if one of us put up an antelope, or had a chance at one when driven by the dogs, he would always fire, and the pack were saved from the ill effects of total discouragement by so often getting these wounded beasts. It was astonishing to see how fast an antelope with a broken leg could run. If such a beast had a good start, and especially if the dogs were tired, it would often lead them a hard chase, and the dogs would be utterly exhausted after it had been killed; so that we would have to let them lie where they were for a long time before trying to lead them down to some stream-bed. If possible, we carried water for them in canteens.

There were red-letter days, however, in which our dogs fairly ran down and killed antelope,—days when the weather was cool, and when it happened that we got our dogs out to the ground without their being tired by previous runs, and found our quarry soon, and in favorable places for slipping the hounds. I remember one such chase in particular. We had at the time a mixed pack, in which there was only one dog of my own, the others being contributed from various sources. It included two greyhounds, a rough-coated deerhound, a foxhound, and the fawn-colored crossbred mentioned above.

We rode out in the early morning, the dogs trotting behind us; and, coming to a low tract of rolling hills, just at the edge of the great prairie, we separated and rode over the crest of the nearest ridge. Just as we topped it, a fine buck leaped up from a hollow a hundred yards off, and turned to look at us for a moment. All the dogs were instantly spinning toward him down the grassy slope. He apparently saw those at the right, and, turning, raced away from us in a diagonal line, so that the left-hand greyhound, which ran cunningly and tried to cut him off, was very soon almost alongside. He saw her, however,—she was a very fast bitch,—just in time, and, wheeling, altered his course to the right. As he reached the edge of the prairie, this alteration nearly brought him in contact with the crossbred, which had obtained a rather poor start, on the extreme right of the line. Around went the buck again, evidently panic-struck and puzzled to the last degree, and started straight off across the prairie, the dogs literally at his heels, and we, urging our horses with whip and spur, but a couple of hundred yards behind. For half a mile the pace was tremendous, when one of the greyhounds made a spring at his ear, but, failing to make good his hold, was thrown off. However, it halted the buck for a moment, and made him turn quarter round, and in a second the deerhound had seized him by the flank and thrown him, and all the dogs piled on top, never allowing him to rise.

Later in the day we again put up a buck not far off. At first it went slowly, and the dogs hauled up on it; but when they got pretty close, it seemed to see them, and letting itself out, went clean away from them almost without effort.

Once or twice we came upon bands of antelope, and the hounds would immediately take after them. I was always rather sorry for this, however, because the frightened animals, as is generally the case when beasts are in a herd, seemed to impede one another, and the chase usually ended by the dogs seizing a doe, for it was of course impossible to direct them to any particular beast.

It will be seen that with us coursing was a homely sport. Nevertheless we had very good fun, and I shall always have enjoyable memories of the rapid gallops across the prairie, on the trail of a flying prongbuck.

Theodore Roosevelt.

After Wapiti in Wyoming

I went into camp, one night in September, on one of the many branches of the upper Snake River, in northwestern Wyoming. It was after a most severe and perplexing day's pack,—one of those days in which "things" go wrong. The packs turned, the cinches refused to hold, and the fresh little Indian pony—for which we had traded a sore-backed packhorse, one cup of sugar, and a half-dozen cartridges, three days previous, with some Bannack Indians who came to my camp-fire on the Snake River—fancied she could put everybody in good temper by having a bucking fit. She had managed to settle one side of her pack on a sharp stub when she came down from a flight, and to punch a fair-sized hole in the canvas cover, which immediately began to flow granulated sugar; but by good luck we managed to catch her lariat and rearrange her pack, minus about one half our supply of sweets. The day was finished with eight horses thoroughly tired, and three men in a condition which admitted of only the fewest words with the longest possible intervals between. Gloom overhung the outfit.

These feelings disappeared as soon as we had finished our supper, and we had just lighted our pipes when, close by our camp-fire, we heard clearly the call of a bull elk. Up to that time I had not had a shot at this, the grandest of all the deer family, and I was quickly on my feet, rifle in hand. Wading the brook, I stalked as hurriedly as I dared toward an opening some forty rods beyond. It was just the last glimmer of daylight, and I made time until I came to the bank, over which I could look into the open park where I felt the royal beast was. What a picture greeted my gaze! The park was perhaps four hundred yards across, and nearly oval in shape, and from the opposite side ran out, nearly to the middle, a plateau some thirty feet in height. On the point of this, standing as immovable as one of Barye's bronzes, was a bull elk with antlers that would please the most fastidious sportsman in the world. In a moment he elevated his head and gave a call ending with those liquid flute-notes that make the blood run quickly in the most phlegmatic hunter's veins. A quick glance showed me that I could not approach him any nearer, and putting up my sight, as I thought, high enough, I pressed the trigger, and saw the bullet strike just under his belly. He whirled and made for cover, and out of pure desperation I gave him another shot, without result. In a shorter time than I have spent in telling this, the twilight had entirely disappeared, and I wended my way back to camp with only the memory of what I had seen to repay me for the wetting which my hurried crossing of the brook had given me.

For three days we had climbed mountains, wallowed through mud-holes, and tobogganed down clay banks, hunting for elk which the Indians had frightened away from the Snake River by their noisy mode of hunting. There were four lodges of Bannacks, and they had some eighty horses of various kinds and colors. They said they had spent six weeks there jerking elk-meat for their winter's food. The country which we crossed during these three days was completely checkered with elk trails, mud-wallows, slivered trees, and many other evidences that large bands of elk had occupied the country for months; and my packer insisted that we would surely find them if we continued hunting in the rough mountains which lay to the east.

Early the next day, while at the brook making my morning toilet, I heard Stewart say to the cook that the horses had gone out of the country; and after two minutes of very vehement remarks, he informed me that five horses had taken the back trail, and that Worth must go with him to head them off. So, each taking a horse, they rode away, leaving me to keep camp with only old Scoop Shovel, a split-eared packhorse, for company.

Always having loved nature, I concluded that a little prospecting on my own hook would be preferable to lounging about camp waiting for the return of the men and horses; so, saddling old Scoop Shovel, I forded the brook and, crossing the scene of my bad shooting the previous evening, climbed a small range of hills. On the opposite side I found a good-sized stream, which I thought was the main Coulter Creek. Following it up some two miles, I suddenly heard a bull elk call, and fastening my horse, I crept toward the sound. Coming out of some thick woods, I saw across the stream a band of seven elk and three or four calves. They were feeding away from me, and I decided that if I crossed the stream and reached the top of a little hill before they could walk out of the woods and get into the middle of an open park, some half-mile across, I might be able to get a shot. The stream was quite rapid and fairly deep, and while I did not care for wet feet, I hoped to escape a wet jacket. However, as I stepped boldly in, the current whirled me off my feet, and the water opened its gates and let me find a resting-place on the slippery, smooth stones of its bottom.

On gaining the opposite bank, I broke into a run for my game. I have always been a fair sprinter, but before I had reached the hill, fifty or sixty rods away, I was completely pumped, and had to stop. Fortunately I was running toward game, rather than being chased by a grizzly, for I had shot my bolt. The high altitude had put me out of the race. However, a rest for a few minutes got me in order, and slowly climbing the hill, I looked over and saw that the band, a hundred yards away, had stopped feeding, and with elevated heads were trying to catch the scent of possible danger. I decided to chance a shot, and with lungs well filled covered the bull. At the report, I heard the shot strike, and with three leaps he came to his knees, but only quickly to regain his feet and trot away. I started on the run toward him, and he having then reached the brook, leaped for the opposite bank. Firing while he was in the air, I saw him fall on his head on landing, and hurried up just as he was having his last struggle. My first shot had been too far back; the second went in at the flank, ranging forward and breaking his shoulder.

His harem were somewhat dazed, and did not evince much fear, but stood crowded together looking at me. I shouted at them, and as that did not frighten them away, waved my hat and walked toward the band; they only trotted a few yards and halted, facing me. I then fired a shot over their heads, and running at full speed toward them, they broke into a trot, crossed a small piece of thin timber, slowed down to a walk, crossed the open park, and, occasionally stopping to look back, finally disappeared up the mountain-side. The bull was a magnificent specimen, with a head royal, twelve good points, and remarkably even and symmetrical. I killed other bulls with more points, but none which was in all respects so perfect as this.

The next night I camped within two hundred yards of this elk, and was awakened by hearing some large animal feeding on his carcass; but the night was dark, and as I was without any light but firebrands, I did not make the attempt to see if it was a grizzly—which the next day proved it to have been. I asked my packer if he wanted to go and interview the visitor; he said he had not lost any grizzlies, and we concluded that our blankets were more comfortable than the unknown quantity of a grizzly in the dark.

The next day, on Piñon Mountain, hearing several bulls call from the same place, I stalked the band and counted thirty-odd head, with five bulls in sight, all within eighty yards. With my glass I counted the points on each head, and selecting the finest, fired but one shot, and the bull did not go more than twenty feet before falling. I think, with my repeating-rifle, I could have killed three or four more, but I refrained from doing so; in fact, I did not kill a cow during the trip. The band did not go far; for, while skinning out this head, I could hear the bulls call within a few hundred yards down the mountain-side. I spent two days in the little park at the foot of Piñon Mountain, and saw and heard a great many elk, in bands of three to thirty, but refrained from shooting. Bear signs were fairly abundant; but I did not see a single live bear then. Later, I saw a fine one inside the Yellowstone Park line; and as I had promised Captain Harris I would not shoot inside the park, I told the bear to move on, which he did at a particularly slow pace. This was a black bear; possibly a grizzly would have been more neighborly.

I enjoyed one triumph over my men, who, with the usual freedom of Westerners, had dubbed me "Pilgrim"—Stewart, in particular, fancied a man from the East could not teach him anything regarding sport. One Sunday morning he said he would go out and catch a string of trout, that we might have a change of diet. He spent an hour and a half at the brook, and returned with one small Rocky Mountain trout, about four inches in length, saying there were plenty of trout, but they were so wild he could not catch them. I had noticed, on crossing the brook, that the fish would run for a hiding-place, being easily frightened; so, after he had exhausted all his art, I said I would try them. With a fish-pole, a brown hackle, and a bit of elk-meat on the point of the hook, I crawled through the grass, and without showing myself, snapped my fly on to the water, felt a pull, and whisked out a trout. I continued my practice until I had all I wanted, and returned to camp, remarking to the cook as I threw them down:

"Stewart don't know anything about fishing; he ought to take some lessons. There are plenty of trout in the brook only waiting to be caught"; which piqued Stewart so much that he sulked for the balance of the day, highly displeased at being beaten by a tenderfoot at the simple game of fishing.

Northwestern Wyoming is a magnificent country, and the weather equals the country. On our trip we had but two hours' rain; at night the thermometer went below freezing, but during the middle of the day it ran as high as seventy. One of the curious facts is that the elk trails could not be better located by human mind or hand to overcome the difficulties of the broken country, and they are used almost entirely by hunters and pack-trains in passing from one point to another. The elk has an eye to the beautiful as well, for I often found well-beaten lookouts on the extreme edge of precipices, showing that they enjoy resting at these points to view the beautiful scenery. It was a veritable paradise for big game, and there must have been hundreds of elk within a few miles of my camp. There was some sign of moose, and the Bannack Indians told me that they had killed one with "heap big horns."

Much against my wishes we decided to break camp and move north, when from the Piñon Mountain we could see the higher peaks north of us covered with snow; for we feared that we might be caught by a heavy snowfall, and have trouble in getting out. My intention was to have gone south to Buffalo Fork, looking for bear, but this I was obliged to postpone to some future date; so we bade good-by to the charming little park where we were camped, and journeyed north, lowering our altitude many hundred feet as we dropped down on the head waters of the next creek. Its valley and the surrounding mountains were as well supplied with elk as the country from which we had just come. I saw bear signs quite frequently, and many of them fresh, but did not spend much time looking for the animal, as I found the usual and most successful way was to bait with an elk carcass and watch through the day, hoping that a bear would scent the bait and come to feed on the flesh. This is slow business, and I preferred more activity. One night I distinctly heard the cry of a mountain-lion, or panther, several times.

Going up Snake River, I passed within the boundaries of the park, and camped one night close by a little pond just under Mount Sheridan, some two miles south of Heart Lake. As I was eating my supper, half an hour before sunset, a fine band of elk came out on the mossy shores of the pond and frisked and played for some time. The old bull would hook and prod the cows, and occasionally call, getting answers from nearly every point of the compass. The next day we skirted Heart Lake on the westerly side as far as the inlet, then through and over the curious hot-spring formation for a couple of miles.

Heart Lake is a charming sheet of water, nestling as it does among these heavily timbered mountains, and it is said to have an abundance of fine trout. While riding along the shore I often saw a good-sized fish shoot from the shallow out into deep water. There were a great many ducks and geese in and about the inlet, and one flock of geese offered a most tempting shot. My pack from Heart Lake to the Hot Springs on the shores of Yellowstone Lake was very tedious, as we found no drinking-water on the trail. The day was warm, and I looked forward to my arrival at Yellowstone Lake with anticipated pleasure in the drink of spring water which I was to have that night; but on arriving I found the spring dried up and nothing but lake water to drink. That was warm, with a sulphurous flavor, owing to the hot springs close by the shore and under the water as well, besides holding many wigglers. I strained a bottleful of water through some linen and hung it on the limb of a tree, waiting for it to cool, and looking at it with the hungry eye of a wolf watching meat hung out of reach.

My Indian pony had a new experience the following morning. After starting our pack-train, we skirted the shores of Yellowstone Lake, and coming to a quick-running stream, which in its clearness looked very inviting, the Indian pony succeeded in loosing her trail-rope, and pushed her head nearly up to her eyes into this clear water. Withdrawing it quickly with a scream, she cut such capers that for a while our pack-train was more or less disarranged. The water had run only a short distance from a boiling spring, and the heat had taken off a good deal of the hair from her face. For twenty-four hours I could not induce her to drink.

On the trail to the outlet of Yellowstone Lake, I saw several bands of elk, and rode within thirty yards of them. They did not show signs of fear, but quietly walked off into the bushes, with the exception of one bull accompanied by three cows. They were lying down, and when I came to them, the cows moved off; but the bull stood there, and for a few minutes I thought he was going to charge. He pawed the ground, shook his head, and kept alternately taking a few steps toward me, and then backing a little, ripping up the soil with his antlers, and breaking the small bushes, in token of challenge. I concluded to retreat rather than fight, so quietly withdrew, leaving him in possession of the field.

While in camp one day, on Lizard Creek, I climbed Wild Cat Mountain, hunting up a trail that would lead to the eastward; and coming out on the southern point of the mountain, a magnificent view opened to my gaze. On the south, immediately at the foot of this mountain, was a park; it was dotted with clumps and groves of fine trees, through which ran a good-sized stream. The meadow ran a half-mile to the foot-hills, well covered with long grass, which in the sunlight, moving with a gentle breeze, rose and fell like the billows of the ocean. For miles beyond were mountains piled on mountains; and I could see clearly the grand Teton range springing up from Jackson's Lake: Mount Hayden, some fourteen thousand feet high, with Mount Moran just north of it,—Hayden rising majestically from the surface of the lake thousands of feet, with sharp slopes and walls of bare rock above, and its base buried in a darkness of pine and spruce. Their snow-covered summits and immense glaciers must impress any beholder with a strong sense of sublimity. It is said that on the summit of one of the Tetons there is an inclosure made of rocks several feet in height, built by what long-vanished and forgotten race of builders no man will ever know.

F. C. Crocker.

In Buffalo Days

On the floor, on either side of my fireplace, lie two buffalo skulls. They are white and weathered, the horns cracked and bleached by the snows and frosts and the rains and heats of many winters and summers. Often, late at night, when the house is quiet, I sit before the fire, and muse and dream of the old days; and as I gaze at these relics of the past, they take life before my eyes. The matted brown hair again clothes the dry bone, and in the empty orbits the wild eyes gleam. Above me curves the blue arch; away on every hand stretches the yellow prairie, and scattered near and far are the dark forms of buffalo. They dot the rolling hills, quietly feeding like tame cattle, or lie at ease on the slopes, chewing the cud and half asleep. The yellow calves are close by their mothers; on little eminences the great bulls paw the dust, and mutter and moan, while those whose horns have grown one, two, and three winters are mingled with their elders.

Not less peaceful is the scene near some river-bank, when the herds come down to water. From the high prairie on every side they stream into the valley, stringing along in single file, each band following the deep trail worn in the parched soil by the tireless feet of generations of their kind. At a quick walk they swing along, their heads held low. The long beards of the bulls sweep the ground; the shuffling tread of many hoofs marks their passing, and above each long line rises a cloud of dust that sometimes obscures the westering sun.

Life, activity, excitement, mark another memory as vivid as these. From behind a near hill mounted men ride out and charge down toward the herd. For an instant the buffalo pause to stare, and then crowd together in a close throng, jostling and pushing one another, a confused mass of horns, hair, and hoofs. Heads down and tails in air, they rush away from their pursuers, and as they race along herd joins herd, till the black mass sweeping over the prairie numbers thousands. On its skirts hover the active, nimble horsemen, with twanging bowstrings and sharp arrows piercing many fat cows. The naked Indians cling to their naked horses as if the two were parts of one incomparable animal, and swing and yield to every motion of their steeds with the grace of perfect horsemanship. The ponies, as quick and skilful as the men, race up beside the fattest of the herd, swing off to avoid the charge of a maddened cow, and, returning, dart close to the victim, whirling hither and yon, like swallows on the wing. And their riders, with the unconscious skill, grace, and power of matchless archery, are drawing their bows to the arrow's head, and driving the feathered shaft deep through the bodies of the buffalo. Returning on their tracks, they skin the dead, then load the meat and robes on their horses, and with laughter and jest ride away.

After them, on the deserted prairie, come the wolves to tear at the carcasses. The rain and the snow wash the blood from the bones, and fade and bleach the hair. For a few months the skeleton holds together; then it falls apart, and the fox and the badger pull about the whitening bones and scatter them over the plain. So this cow and this bull of mine may have left their bones on the prairie, where I found them and picked them up to keep as mementos of the past, to dream over, and in such reverie to see again the swelling hosts which yesterday covered the plains, and to-day are but a dream.

So the buffalo passed into history. Once an inhabitant of this continent from the Arctic slope to Mexico, and from Virginia to Oregon, and, within the memory of men yet young, roaming the plains in such numbers that it seemed as if it could never be exterminated, it has now disappeared as utterly as has the bison from Europe. For it is probable that the existing herds of that practically extinct species, now carefully guarded in the forests of Grodno, about equal in numbers the buffalo in the Yellowstone Park; while the wild bison in the Caucasus may be compared with the "wood" buffalo which survive in the Peace River district. In view of the former abundance of our buffalo, this parallel is curious and interesting.

The early explorers were constantly astonished by the multitudinous herds which they met with, the regularity of their movements, and the deep roads which they made in traveling from place to place. Many of the earlier references are to territory east of the Mississippi, but even within the last fifteen years buffalo were to be seen on the Western plains in numbers so great that an entirely sober and truthful account seems like fable. Describing the abundance of buffalo in a certain region, an Indian once said to me, in the expressive sign-language of which all old frontiersmen have some knowledge: "The country was one robe."

Much has been written about their enormous abundance in the old days, but I have never read anything that I thought an exaggeration of their numbers as I have seen them. Only one who has actually spent months in traveling among them in those old days can credit the stories told about them. The trains of the Kansas Pacific Railroad used frequently to be detained by herds which were crossing the tracks in front of the engines; and in 1870, trains on which I was traveling were twice so held, in one case for three hours. When railroad travel first began on this road, the engineers tried the experiment of running through these passing herds; but after their engines had been thrown from the tracks they learned wisdom, and gave the buffalo the right of way. Two or three years later, in the country between the Platte and Republican rivers, I saw a closely massed herd of buffalo so vast that I dared not hazard a guess as to its numbers; and in later years I have traveled, for weeks at a time, in northern Montana without ever being out of sight of buffalo. These were not in close herds, except now and then when alarmed and running, but were usually scattered about, feeding or lying down on the prairie at a little distance from one another, much as domestic cattle distribute themselves in a pasture or on the range. As far as we could see on every side of the line of march, and ahead, the hillsides were dotted with dark forms, and the field-glass revealed yet others stretched out on every side, in one continuous host, to the most distant hills. Thus was gained a more just notion of their numbers than could be had in any other way, for the sight of this limitless territory occupied by these continuous herds was far more impressive than the spectacle of a surging, terrified mass of fleeing buffalo, even though the numbers which passed rapidly before the observer's gaze in a short time were very great.

At Mid-day.
From Scribner's Magazine.

The former range of the buffalo has been worked out with painstaking care by Dr. Allen, to whom we owe an admirable monograph on this species. He concludes that the northern limit of this range was north of the Great Slave Lake, in latitude about 63° N.; while to the south it extended into Mexico as far as latitude 25° N. To the west it ranged at least as far as the Blue Mountains of Oregon, while on the east it was abundant in the western portions of New York, Pennsylvania, Virginia, North and South Carolinas, and Georgia. In the interior the buffalo were very abundant, and occupied Ohio, Kentucky, West Virginia, Tennessee, West Georgia, Illinois, Indiana, and Iowa, parts of Michigan, Wisconsin, and Minnesota, the whole of the great plains, from southern Texas north to their northern limit, and much of the Rocky Mountains. In Montana, Idaho, Wyoming, and most of New Mexico they were abundant, and probably common over a large part of Utah, and perhaps in northern Nevada. So far as now known, their western limit was the Blue Mountains of Oregon and the eastern foothills of the Sierra Nevada.

Thus it will be seen that the buffalo once ranged over a large part of the American continent,—Dr. Allen says one third of it,—but it must not be imagined that they were always present at the same time in every part of their range. They were a wandering race, sometimes leaving a district and being long absent, and again returning and occupying it for a considerable period. What laws or what impulses governed these movements we cannot know. Their wandering habits were well understood by the Indians of the Western plains, who depended upon the buffalo for food. It was their custom to follow the herds about, and when, as sometimes occurred, these moved away and could not be found, the Indians were reduced to great straits for food, and sometimes even starved to death.

Under natural conditions the buffalo was an animal of rather sluggish habits, mild, inoffensive, and dull. In its ways of life and intelligence it closely resembled our domestic cattle. It was slow to learn by experience, and this lack of intelligence greatly hastened the destruction of the race. Until the very last years of its existence as a species, it did not appear to connect the report of firearms with any idea of danger to itself, and though constantly pursued, did not become wild. If he used skill and judgment in shooting, a hunter who had "got a stand" on a small bunch could kill them all before they had moved out of rifle-shot. It was my fortune, one summer, to hunt for a camp of soldiers, and more than once I have lain on a hill above a little herd of buffalo, shot down what young bulls I needed to supply the camp, and then walked down to the bunch and, by waving my hat and shouting, driven off the survivors, so that I could prepare the meat for transportation to camp. This slowness to take the alarm, or indeed to realize the presence of danger, was characteristic of the buffalo almost up to the very last. A time did come when they were alarmed readily enough, but this was not until all the large herds had been broken up and scattered, and the miserable survivors had been so chased and harried that at last they learned to start and run even at their own shadows.

Another peculiarity of the buffalo was its habit, when stampeded, of dashing blindly forward against, over, or through anything that might be in the way. When running, a herd of buffalo followed its leaders, and yet these leaders lost the power of stopping, or even of turning aside, because they were constantly crowded upon and pushed forward by those behind. This explains why herds would dash into mire or quicksands, as they often did, and thus perish by the thousand. Those in front could not stop, while those behind could not see the danger toward which they were rushing. So, too, they ran into rivers, or into traps made for them by the Indians, or against railroad cars, or even dashed into the rivers and swam blindly against the sides of steamboats. If an obstacle lay squarely across their path, they tried to go through it, but if it lay at an angle to their course, they would turn a little to follow it, as will be shown further on.

The buffalo calf is born from April to June, and at first is an awkward little creature, looking much like a domestic calf, but with a shorter neck. The hump at first is scarcely noticeable, but develops rapidly. They are odd-looking and very playful little animals. They are easily caught and tamed when quite young, but when a few months old they become as shy as the old buffalo, and are much more swift of foot.

Although apparently very sluggish, buffalo are really extremely active, and are able to go at headlong speed over a country where no man would dare to ride a horse. When alarmed they will throw themselves down the almost vertical side of a cañon and climb the opposite wall with cat-like agility. Sometimes they will descend cut banks by jumping from shelf to shelf of rock like the mountain sheep. To get at water when thirsty, they will climb down bluffs that seem altogether impracticable for such great animals. Many years ago, while descending the Missouri River in a flatboat with two companions, I landed in a wide bottom to kill a mountain sheep. As we were bringing the meat to the boat, we saw on the opposite side of the river, about half-way down the bluffs, which were here about fifteen hundred feet high, a large buffalo bull. The bluffs were almost vertical, and this old fellow was having some difficulty in making his way down to the water. He went slowly and carefully, at times having pretty good going, and at others slipping and sliding for thirty or forty feet, sending the clay and stones rolling ahead of him in great quantities. We watched him for a little while, and then it occurred to some malicious spirit among us that it would be fun to see whether the bull could go up where he had come down. A shot was fired so as to strike near him,—for no one wanted to hurt the old fellow,—and as soon as the report reached his ears, he turned about and began to scramble up the bluffs. His first rush carried him, perhaps, a hundred feet vertically, and then he stopped and looked around. He seemed not to have the slightest difficulty in climbing up, nor did he use any caution, or appear to pick his way at all. A second shot caused another rush up the steep ascent, but this time he went only half as far as before, and again stopped. Three or four other shots drove him by shorter and shorter rushes up the bluffs, until at length he would go no further, and subsequent shots only caused him to shake his head angrily. Plainly he had climbed until his wind had given out, and now he would stand and fight. Our fun was over, and looking back as we floated down the river, our last glimpse was of the old bull, still standing on his shelf, waiting with lowered head for the unknown enemy that he supposed was about to attack him.

It is not only under the stress of circumstances that the bison climbs. The mountain buffalo is almost as active as the mountain sheep, and was often found in places that tested the nerve and activity of a man to reach; and even the buffalo of the plains had a fondness for high places, and used to climb up on to broken buttes or high rocky points. In recent years I have often noticed the same habit among range cattle and horses.

The buffalo were fond of rolling in the dirt, and to this habit, practised when the ground was wet, are due the buffalo wallows which so frequently occur in the old ranges, and which often contain water after all other moisture, except that of the streams, is dried up. These wallows were formed by the rolling of a succession of buffalo in the same moist place, and were frequently quite deep. They have often been described. Less well known was the habit of scratching themselves against trees and rocks. Sometimes a solitary erratic boulder, five or six feet high, may be seen on the bare prairie, the ground immediately around it being worn down two or three feet below the level of the surrounding earth. This is where the buffalo have walked about the stone, rubbing against it, and, where they trod, loosening the soil, which has been blown away by the wind, so that in course of time a deep trench was worn about the rock. Often single trees along streams were worn quite smooth by the shoulders and sides of the buffalo.

When the first telegraph line was built across the continent, the poles used were light and small, for transportation over the plains was slow and expensive, and it was not thought necessary to raise the wires high above the ground. These poles were much resorted to by the buffalo to scratch against, and before long a great many of them were pushed over. A story, now of considerable antiquity, is told of an ingenious employee of the telegraph company, who devised a plan for preventing the buffalo from disturbing the poles. This he expected to accomplish by driving into them spikes which should prick the animals when they rubbed against them. The result somewhat astonished the inventor, for it was discovered that where formerly one buffalo rubbed against the smooth telegraph poles, ten now struggled and fought for the chance to scratch themselves against the spiked poles, the iron furnishing just the irritation which their tough hides needed.

It was in spring, when its coat was being shed, that the buffalo, odd-looking enough at any time, presented its most grotesque appearance. The matted hair and wool of the shoulders and sides began to peel off in great sheets, and these sheets, clinging to the skin and flapping in the wind, gave it the appearance of being clad in rags.

The buffalo was a timid creature, but brought to bay would fight with ferocity. There were few sights more terrifying to the novice than the spectacle of an old bull at bay: his mighty bulk, a quivering mass of active, enraged muscle; the shining horns; the little, spiky tail; and the eyes half hidden beneath the shaggy frontlet, yet gleaming with rage, combined to render him an awe-inspiring object. Nevertheless, owing to their greater speed and activity, the cows were much more to be feared than the bulls.

It was once thought that the buffalo performed annually extensive migrations, and it was even said that those which spent the summer on the banks of the Saskatchewan wintered in Texas. There is no reason for believing this to have been true. Undoubtedly there were slight general movements north and south, and east and west, at certain seasons of the year; but many of the accounts of these movements are entirely misleading, because greatly exaggerated. In one portion of the northern country I know that there was a decided east and west seasonal migration, the herds tending in spring away from the mountains, while in the autumn they worked back again, seeking shelter in the rough, broken country of the foot-hills from the cold west winds of the winter.

The buffalo is easily tamed when caught as a calf, and in all its ways of life resembles the domestic cattle. It at once learns to respect a fence, and, even if at large, manifests no disposition to wander.

Three years ago there were in this country about two hundred and fifty domesticated buffalo, in the possession of about a dozen individuals. Of these the most important herd was that of Hon. C. J. Jones, of Garden City, Kansas, which, besides about fifty animals captured and reared by himself, included also the Bedson herd of over eighty, purchased in Manitoba. The Jones herd at one time consisted of about one hundred and fifty head. Next came that of Charles Allard and Michel Pablo, of the Flathead Agency in Montana, which in 1888 numbered thirty-five, and has now increased to about ninety. Mr. Jones's herd has been broken up, and he now retains only about forty-five head, of which fifteen are breeding cows. He tells me that within the past year or two he has sold over sixty pure buffalo, and that nearly as many more have died through injuries received in transporting them by rail.

Mr. Jones is the only individual who, of recent years, has made any systematic effort to cross the buffalo with our own domestic cattle. As far back as the beginning of the present century, this was successfully done in the West and Northwest; and in Audubon and Bachman's "Quadrupeds of America" may be found an extremely interesting account, written by Robert Wickliffe, of Lexington, Kentucky, giving the results of a series of careful and successful experiments which he carried on for more than thirty years. These experiments showed that the cross for certain purposes was a very valuable one, but no systematic efforts to establish and perpetuate a breed of buffalo cattle were afterward made until within the past ten years. Mr. Jones has bred buffalo bulls to Galloway, Polled Angus, and ordinary range cows, and has succeeded in obtaining calves from all. Such half-breeds are of very large size, extremely hardy, and, as a farmer would say, "easy keepers." They are fertile among themselves or with either parent. A half-breed cow of Mr. Jones's that I examined was fully as large as an ordinary work-ox, and in spring, while nursing a calf, was fat on grass. She lacked the buffalo hump, but her hide would have made a good robe. The great size and tremendous frame of these crossbred cattle should make them very valuable for beef, while their hardiness would exempt them from the dangers of winter,—so often fatal to domestic range cattle,—and they produce a robe which is quite as valuable as that of the buffalo, and more beautiful because more even all over. If continued, these attempts at cross-breeding may do much to improve our Western range cattle.

Mr. Jones has sold a number of buffalo to persons in Europe, where there is a considerable demand for them. It is to be hoped that no more of these domesticated buffalo will be allowed to leave the country where they were born. Indeed, it would seem quite within the lines of the work now being carried on by the Agricultural Department, for the government to purchase all the domesticated American buffalo that can be had, and to start, in some one of the Western States, an experimental farm for buffalo breeding and buffalo crossing. With a herd of fifty pure-bred buffalo cows and a sufficient number of bulls, a series of experiments could be carried on which might be of great value to the cattle-growers of our western country. The stock of pure buffalo could be kept up and increased; surplus bulls, pure and half bred, could be sold to farmers; and, in time, the new race of buffalo cattle might become so firmly established that it would endure.

To undertake this with any prospect of success, such a farm would have to be managed by a man of intelligence and of wide experience in this particular field; otherwise all the money invested would be wasted. Mr. Jones is perhaps the only man living who knows enough of this subject to carry on an experimental farm with success.

Although only one species of buffalo is known to science, old mountaineers and Indians tell of four kinds. These are, besides the ordinary animal of the plains, the "mountain buffalo," sometimes called "bison," which is found in the timbered Rocky Mountains; the "wood buffalo" of the Northwest, which inhabits the timbered country to the west and north of Athabasca Lake; and the "beaver buffalo." The last named has been vaguely described to me by northern Indians as small and having a very curly coat. I know of only one printed account of it, and this says that it had "short, sharp horns which were small at the root and curiously turned up and bent backward, not unlike a ram's, but quite unlike the bend of the horn in the common buffalo." It is possible that this description may refer to the musk-ox, and not to a buffalo. The "mountain" and "wood" buffalo seem to be very much alike in habit and appearance. They are larger, darker, and heavier than the animal of the plains, but there is no reason for thinking them specifically distinct from it. Such differences as exist are due to conditions of environment.

The color of the buffalo in its new coat is a dark liver-brown. This soon changes, however, and the hides, which are at their best in November and early December, begin to grow paler toward spring; and when the coat is shed, the hair and wool from young animals is almost a dark smoky-gray. The calf when just born is of a bright yellow color, almost a pale red on the line of the back. As it grows older it becomes darker, and by late autumn is almost as dark as the adults. Variations from the normal color are very rare, but pied, spotted, and roan animals are sometimes killed. Blue or mouse-colored buffalo were occasionally seen, and a bull of this color was observed in the National Park last January. White buffalo—though often referred to as mythical—sometimes occurred. These varied from gray to cream-white. The rare and valuable "silk" or "beaver" robe owes its name to its dark color and its peculiar sheen or gloss. White or spotted robes were highly valued by the Indians. Among the Blackfeet they were presented to the Sun as votive offerings. Other tribes kept them in their sacred bundles.

Apart from man, the buffalo had but few natural enemies. Of these the most destructive were the wolves, which killed a great many of them. These, however, were principally old, straggling bulls, for the calves were protected by their mothers, and the females and young stock were so vigorous and so gregarious that they had but little to fear from this danger. It is probable that, notwithstanding the destruction which they wrought, the wolves performed an important service for the buffalo race, keeping it vigorous and healthy by killing weak, disabled, and superannuated animals, which could no longer serve any useful purpose in the herd, and yet consumed the grass which would support a healthy breeding animal. It is certainly true that sick buffalo, or those out of condition, were rarely seen.

The grizzly bear fed to some extent on the carcasses of buffalo drowned in the rivers or caught in the quicksands, and occasionally they caught living buffalo and killed them. A Blackfoot Indian told me of an attempt of this kind which he witnessed. He was lying hidden by a buffalo trail in the Bad Lands, near a little creek, waiting for a small bunch to come down to water, so that he might kill one. The buffalo came on in single file as usual, the leading animal being a young heifer. When they had nearly reached the water, and were passing under a vertical clay wall, a grizzly bear, lying hid on a shelf of this wall, reached down, and with both paws caught the heifer about the neck and threw himself upon her. The others at once ran off, and a short struggle ensued, the bear trying to kill the heifer, and she to escape. Almost at once, however, the Indian saw a splendid young bull come rushing down the trail toward the scene of conflict, and charge the bear, knocking him down. A fierce combat ensued. The bull would charge the bear, and when he struck him fairly would knock him off his feet, often inflicting severe wounds with his sharp horns. The bear struck at the bull, and tried to catch him by the head or shoulders, and to hold him, but this he could not do. After fifteen or twenty minutes of fierce and active fighting, the bear had received all the punishment he cared for, and tried to escape, but the bull would not let him go, and kept up the attack until he had killed his adversary. Even after the bear was dead the bull would gore the carcass and sometimes lift it clear of the ground on his horns. He seemed insane with rage, and, notwithstanding the fact that most of the skin was torn from his head and shoulders, appeared to be looking about for something else to fight. The Indian was very much afraid lest the bull should discover and kill him, and was greatly relieved when he finally left the bear and went off to join his band. This Blackfoot had never heard of Uncle Remus's tales, but he imitated Brer Rabbit—laid low and said nothing.

To the Indians the buffalo was the staff of life. It was their food, clothing, dwellings, tools. The needs of a savage people are not many, perhaps, but whatever the Indians of the plains had, that the buffalo gave them. It is not strange, then, that this animal was revered by most plains tribes, nor that it entered largely into their sacred ceremonies, and was in a sense worshiped by them. The Pawnees, in explaining their religious customs, say, "Through the corn and the buffalo we worship the Father." The Blackfeet ask, "What one of all the animals is most sacred?" and the reply given is, "The buffalo."

The robe was the Indian's winter covering and his bed, while the skin, freed from the hair and dressed, constituted his summer sheet or blanket. The dressed hide was used for moccasins, leggings, shirts, and women's dresses. Dressed cow-skins formed the lodges, the warmest and most comfortable portable shelters ever devised. Braided strands of rawhide furnished them with ropes and lines, and these were made also from the twisted hair. The green hide was sometimes used as a kettle, in which to boil meat, or, stretched over a frame of boughs, gave them coracles, or boats, for crossing rivers. The tough, thick hide of the bull's neck, allowed to shrink smooth, made a shield which would turn a lance-thrust, an arrow, or even the ball from an old-fashioned smooth-bore gun. From the rawhide, the hair having been shaved off, were made parfleches—envelop-like cases which served for trunks or boxes—useful to contain small articles. The cannon-bones and ribs were used to make implements for dressing hides; the shoulder-blades lashed to sticks made hoes and axes, and the ribs runners for small sledges drawn by dogs. The hoofs were boiled to make a glue for fastening the feathers and heads on their arrows, the hair used to stuff cushions, and later saddles, strands of the long black beard to ornament articles of wearing-apparel and implements of war, such as shields and quivers. The sinews lying along the back gave them thread and bowstrings, and backed their bows. The horns furnished spoons and ladles, and ornamented their war-bonnets. Water-buckets were made from the lining of the paunch. The skin of the hind leg cut off above the pastern, and again a short distance above the hock, was once used for a moccasin or boot. Fly-brushes were made from the skin of the tail dried on sticks. Knife-sheaths, quivers, bow-cases, gun-covers, saddle-cloths, and a hundred other useful and necessary articles, all were furnished by the buffalo.

The Indians killed some smaller game, as elk, deer, and antelope, but for food their dependence was on the buffalo. But before the coming of the whites their knives and arrowheads were merely sharpened stones, weapons which would be inefficient against such great, thick-skinned beasts. Even under the most favorable circumstances, with these primitive implements, they could not kill food in quantities sufficient to supply their needs. There must be some means of taking the buffalo in considerable numbers. Such wholesale capture was accomplished by means of traps or surrounds, which all depended for success on one characteristic of the animal, its curiosity.

The Blackfeet, Plains Crees, Gros Ventres of the Prairie, Sarcees, some bands of the Dakotas, Snakes, Crows, and some others, drove the herds of buffalo into pens from above, or over high cliffs, where the fall killed or crippled a large majority of the herd. The Cheyennes and Arapahoes drove them into pens on level ground; the Blackfeet, Aricaras, Mandans, Gros Ventres of the Village, Pawnees, Omahas, Otoes, and others, surrounded the herds in great circles on the prairie, and then, frightening them so that they started running, kept them from breaking through the line of men, and made them race round and round in a circle, until they were so exhausted that they could not run away, and were easily killed.

These primitive modes of slaughter have been described by earlier writers, and frequently quoted in recent years; yet, in all that has been written on this subject, I fail to find a single account which gives at all a true notion of the methods employed, or the means by which the buffalo were brought into the inclosures. Eye-witnesses have been careless observers, and have taken many things for granted. My understanding of this matter is derived from men who from childhood have been familiar with these things, and from them, during years of close association, I have again and again heard the story of these old hunting methods.

The Blackfoot trap was called the *piskŭ*. It was an inclosure, one side of which was formed by the vertical wall of a cut bank, the others being built of rocks, logs, poles, and brush six or eight feet high. It was not necessary that these walls should be very strong, but they had to be tight, so that the buffalo could not see through them. From a point on the cut bank above this inclosure, in two diverging lines stretching far out into the prairie, piles of rock were heaped up at short intervals, or bushes were stuck in the ground, forming the wings of a V-shaped chute, which would guide any animals running down the chute to its angle above the piskun. When a herd of buffalo were feeding near at hand, the people prepared for the hunt, in which almost the whole camp took part. It is commonly stated that the buffalo were driven into the piskun by mounted men, but this was not the case. They were not driven, but led, and they were led by an appeal to their curiosity. The man who brought them was usually the possessor of a "buffalo rock," a talisman which was believed to give him greater power to call the buffalo than was had by others. The previous night was spent by this man in praying for success in the enterprise of the morrow. The help of the Sun, *Napi,* and all Above People was asked for, and sweet-grass was burned to them. Early in the morning, without eating or drinking, the man started away from the camp and went up on the prairie. Before he left the lodge, he told his wives that they must not go out, or even look out, of the lodge during his

**Blackfoot Indian Pis´kun.
From Scribner's Magazine.**

absence. They should stay there, and pray to the Sun for his success, and burn sweet-grass until he returned. When he left the camp and went up on to the prairie toward the buffalo, all the people followed him, and distributed themselves along the wings of the chute, hiding behind the piles of rock or brush. The caller sometimes wore a robe and a bull's-head bonnet, or at times was naked. When he had approached close to the buffalo, he endeavored to attract their attention by moving about, wheeling round and round, and alternately appearing and disappearing. The feeding buffalo soon began to raise their heads and stare at him, and presently the nearest ones would walk toward him to discover what this strange creature might be, and the others would follow. As they began to approach, the man withdrew toward the entrance of the chute. If the buffalo began to trot, he increased his speed, and before very long he had the herd well within the wings. As soon as they had passed the first piles of rock, behind which some of the people were concealed, the Indians sprang into view, and by yelling and waving robes frightened the hind-most of the buffalo, which then began to run down the chute. As they passed along, more and more people showed themselves and added to their terror, and in a very short time the herd was in a headlong stampede, guided toward the angle above the piskun by the piles of rock on either side.

About the walls of the piskun, now full of buffalo, were distributed the women and children of the camp, who, leaning over the inclosure, waving their arms and calling out, did all they could to frighten the penned-in animals, and to keep them from pushing against the walls or trying to jump or climb over them. As a rule the buffalo raced round within the inclosure, and the men shot them down as they passed, until all were killed. After this the people all entered the piskun and cut up the dead, transporting the meat to camp. The skulls, bones, and less perishable offal were removed from the inclosure, and the wolves, coyotes, foxes, and badgers devoured what was left.

It occasionally happened that something occurred to turn the buffalo, so that they passed through the guiding arms and escaped. Usually they went on straight to the angle and jumped over the cliff into the inclosure below. In winter, when snow was on the ground, their straight course was made additionally certain by placing on, or just above, the snow a line of buffalo-chips leading from the angle of the V, midway between its arms, out on to the prairie. These dark objects, only twenty or thirty feet apart, were easily seen against the white snow, and the buffalo always followed them, no doubt thinking this a trail where another herd had passed.

By the *Siksikau* tribe of the Blackfoot nation and the Plains Crees, the piskun was built in a somewhat different way, but the methods employed were similar. With these people, who inhabited a flat country, the inclosure was built of logs and near a timbered stream. Its circular wall was complete; that is, there was no opening or gateway in it, but at one point this wall, elsewhere eight feet high, was cut away so that its height was only four feet. From this point a bridge or causeway of logs, covered with dirt, sloped by a gradual descent down to the level of the prairie. This bridge was fenced on either side with logs, and the arms of the V came together at the point where the bridge reached the ground. The buffalo were driven down the chute as before, ran up on this bridge, and were forced to leap into the pen. As soon as all had entered, Indians who had been concealed near by ran up and put poles across the opening through which the buffalo had passed, and over these poles hung robes so as entirely to conceal the outer world. Then the butchering of the animals took place.

Further to the south, out on the prairie, where timber and rocks and brush were not obtainable for making traps like these, simpler but less effective methods were adopted. The people would go out on the prairie and conceal themselves in a great circle, open on one side. Then some man would approach the buffalo, and decoy them into the circle. Men would now show themselves at different points and start the buffalo running in a circle, yelling and waving robes to keep them from approaching or trying to break through the ring of men. This had to be done with great judgment, however; for often if the herd got started in one direction it was impossible to turn it, and it would rush through the ring and none would be secured. Sometimes, if a herd was found in a favorable position, and there was no wind, a large camp of people would set up their lodges all about the buffalo, in which case the chances of success in the surround were greatly increased.

The tribes which used the piskun also practised driving the buffalo over high, rough cliffs, where the fall crippled or killed most of the animals which went over. In such situations, no inclosure was built at the foot of the precipice.

In the later days of the piskun in the north, the man who brought the buffalo often went to them on horseback, riding a white horse. He would ride backward and forward before them, zigzagging this way and that, and after a little they would follow him. He never attempted to drive, but always led them. The driving began only after the herd had passed the outer rock piles, and the people had begun to rise up and frighten them.

This method of securing meat has been practised in Montana within thirty years, and even more recently among the Plains Crees of the north. I have seen the remains of old piskuns, and the guiding wings of the chute, and have talked with many men who have taken part in such killings.

All this had to do, of course, with the primitive methods of buffalo killing. As soon as horses became abundant, and sheet-iron arrow-heads and, later, guns were secured by the Indians, these old practices began to give way to the more exciting pursuit of running buffalo and of surrounding them on horseback. Of this modern method, as practised twenty years ago, and exclusively with the bow and arrow, I have already written at some length in another place.

To the white travelers on the plains in early days the buffalo furnished support and sustenance. Their abundance made fresh meat easily obtainable, and the early travelers usually carried with them bundles of dried meat, or sacks of pemmican, food made from the flesh of the buffalo, that contained a great deal of nutriment in very small bulk. Robes were used for bedding, and in winter buffalo moccasins were worn for warmth, the hair side within. Coats of buffalo-skin are the warmest covering known, the only garment which will present an effective barrier to the bitter blasts that sweep over the plains of the Northwest.

Perhaps as useful to early travelers as any product of the buffalo, was the "buffalo chip," or dried dung. This, being composed of comminuted woody fiber of the grass, made an excellent fuel, and in many parts of the treeless plains was the only substance which could be used to cook with.

The dismal story of the extermination of the buffalo for its hides has been so often told, that I may be spared the sickening details of the butchery which was carried on from the Mexican to the British boundary line in the struggle to obtain a few dollars by a most ignoble means. As soon as railroads penetrated the buffalo country, a market was opened for the hides. Men too lazy to work were not too lazy to hunt, and a good hunter could kill in the early days from thirty to seventy-five buffalo a day, the hides of which were worth from $1.50 to $4 each. This seemed an easy way to make money, and the market for hides was unlimited. Up to this time the trade in robes had been mainly confined to those dressed by the Indians, and these were for the most part taken from cows. The coming of the railroad made hides of all sorts marketable, and even those taken from naked old bulls found a sale at some price. The butchery of buffalo was now something stupendous. Thousands of hunters followed millions of buffalo and destroyed them wherever found and at all seasons of the year. They pursued them during the day, and at night camped at the watering-places, and built lines of fires along the streams, to drive the buffalo back so that they could not drink. It took less than six years to destroy all the buffalo in Kansas, Nebraska, Indian Territory, and northern Texas. The few that were left of the southern herd retreated to the waterless plains of Texas, and there for a while had a brief respite. Even here the hunters followed them, but as the animals were few and the territory in which they ranged vast, they held out here for some years. It was in this country, and against the last survivors of this southern herd, that "Buffalo Jones" made his successful trips to capture calves.

The extirpation of the northern herd was longer delayed. No very terrible slaughter occurred until the completion of the Northern Pacific Railroad; then, however, the same scenes of butchery were enacted. Buffalo were shot down by tens of thousands, their hides stripped off, and the meat left to the wolves. The result of the crusade was soon seen, and the last buffalo were killed in the Northwest near the boundary line in 1883, and that year may be said to have finished up the species, though some few were killed in 1884 to 1885.

After the slaughter had been begun, but years before it had been accomplished, the subject was brought to the attention of Congress, and legislation looking to the preservation of the species was urged upon that body. Little general interest was taken in the subject, but in 1874, after much discussion, Congress did pass an act providing for the protection of the buffalo. The bill, however, was never signed by the President.

During the last days of the buffalo, a remarkable change took place in its form, and this change is worthy of consideration by naturalists, for it is an example of specialization—of development in one particular direction—which was due to a change in the environment of the species, and is interesting because it was brought about in a very few years, and indicates how rapidly, under favoring conditions, such specialization may sometimes take place.

This change was noticed and commented on by hunters who followed the northern buffalo, as well as by those who assisted in the extermination of the southern herd. The southern hunters, however, averred that the "regular" buffalo had disappeared—gone off somewhere—and that their place had been taken by what they called the southern buffalo, a race said to have come up from Mexico, and characterized by longer legs and a longer, lighter body than the buffalo of earlier years, and which was also peculiar in that the animals never became fat. Intelligent hunters of the northern herd, however, recognized the true state of the case, which was that the buffalo, during the last years of their existence, were so constantly pursued and driven from place to place that they never had time to lay on fat as in earlier years, and that, as a consequence of this continual running, the animal's form changed, and instead of a fat, short-backed, short-legged animal, it became a long-legged, light-bodied beast, formed for running.

This specialization in the direction of speed at first proceeded very slowly, but at last, as the dangers to which the animals were subjected became more and more pressing, it took place rapidly, and as a consequence the last buffalo killed on the plains were extremely long-legged and rangy, and were very different in appearance—as they were in their habits—from the animals of twenty years ago.

Buffalo running was not a sport that required much skill, yet it was not without its dangers. Occasionally a man was killed by the buffalo, but deaths from falls and from bursting guns were more common. Many curious stories of such accidents are told by the few surviving old-timers whose memory goes back fifty years, to the time when flint-lock guns were in use. A mere fall from a horse is lightly regarded by the practised rider; the danger to be feared is that in such a fall the horse may roll on the man and crush him. Even more serious accidents occurred when a man fell upon some part of his equipment, which was driven through his body. Hunters have fallen in such a way that their whip-stocks, arrows, bows, and even guns, have been driven through their bodies. The old flint-lock guns, or "fukes," which were loaded on the run, with powder poured in from the horn by guess, and a ball from the mouth, used frequently to burst, causing the loss of hands, arms, and even lives.

Through the Mist.
From Scribner's Magazine.

While most of the deaths which occurred in the chase resulted from causes other than the resistance of the buffalo, these did occasionally kill a man. A curious accident happened in a camp of Red River half-breeds in the early seventies. The son of an Iroquois half-breed, about twenty years old, went out one day with the rest of the camp to run buffalo. At night he did not return, and the next day all the men went out to search for him. They found the horse and the arms, but could not find the man, and could not imagine what had become of him. About a year later, as the half-breeds were hunting in another part of the country, a cow was seen which had something unusual on her head. They chased and killed her, and found that she had on her head the pelvis of a man, one of the horns having pierced the thin part of the bone, which was wedged on so tightly that they could hardly get it off. Much of the hair on the head, neck, and shoulders of the cow was worn off short, and on the side on which the bone was, down on the neck and shoulders, the hair was short, black, and looked new, as if it had been worn entirely off the skin, and was just beginning to grow out again. It is supposed that this bone was part of the missing young man, who had been hooked by the cow, and carried about on her head until his body fell to pieces.

My old and valued friend Charles Reynolds, for years chief of scouts at Fort Lincoln, Dakota, and who was killed by the Sioux in the Custer fight in 1876, told me of the death of a hunting partner of his, which shows how dangerous even a dying buffalo may be. The two men had started from the railroad to go south and bring in a load of meat. On finding a bunch of buffalo, they shot down by stalking what they required, and then on foot went up to the animals to skin them. One cow, lying on her side, was still moving a little convulsively, but dying. The man approached her as if about to cut her throat, but when he was within a few feet of her head, she sprang to her feet, rushed at him, struck him in the chest with her horns, and then fell dead. Charley ran up to his partner, and to his horror saw that the cow's horn had ripped him up from the belly to the throat, so that he could see the heart still expanding and contracting.

Charley buried his partner there, and returning to the town, told his story. He was at once arrested on the charge that he had murdered his companion, and was obliged to return to the place and to assist in digging up the body to satisfy the suspicious officials of the truth of his statements.

In the early days, when the game was plenty, buffalo-running was exhilarating sport. Given a good horse, the only other requisite to success was the ability to remain on his back till the end of the chase. No greater degree of skill was needed than this, and yet the quick motion of the horse, the rough ground to be traversed, and the feeling that there was something ahead that must be overtaken and stopped, made the ride attractive. There was the very slightest spice of danger; for while no one anticipated a serious accident, it was always possible that one's horse might step into a badger-hole, in which case his rider would get a fall that would make his bones ache.

The most exciting, and by far the most interesting, hunts in which I ever took part were those with the Indians of the plains. They were conducted almost noiselessly, and no ring of rifle-shot broke the stillness of the air, nor puff of smoke rose toward the still, gray autumn sky. The consummate grace and skill of the naked Indians, and the speed and quickness of their splendid ponies, were well displayed in such chases as these. More than one instance is recorded where an Indian sent an arrow entirely through the bodies of two buffalo. Sometimes such a hunt was signalized by some feat of daring bravado that, save in the seeing, was scarcely credible, as when the Cheyenne Big Ribs rode his horse close up to the side of a huge bull, and, springing on his back, rode the savage beast for some distance, and then with his knife gave him the death-stroke. Or a man might find himself in a position of comical danger, as did "The Trader" who was thrown from his horse on to the horns of a bull without being injured. One of the horns passed under his belt and supported him, and at the same time prevented the bull from tossing him. In this way he was carried for some distance on the animal's head, when the belt gave way and he fell to the ground unhurt, while the bull ran on. There were occasions when buffalo or horses fell in front of horsemen riding at full run, and when a fall was avoided only by leaping one's horse over the fallen animal. In the buffalo chase of old days it was well for a man to keep his wits about him; for, though he might run buffalo a thousand times without accident, the moment might come when only instant action would save him his life, or at least an ugly hurt.

In the early days of the first Pacific Railroad, and before the herds had been driven back from the track, singular hunting-parties were sometimes seen on the buffalo range. These hunters were capitalists connected with the newly constructed road, and some of them now for the first time bestrode a horse, while few had ever used firearms. On such a hunt, one well-known railroad director, eager to kill a buffalo, declined to trust himself on horseback, preferring to bounce over the rough prairie in an ambulance driven by an alarmed soldier, who gave less attention to the mules he was guiding than to the loaded and cocked pistol which his excited passenger was brandishing. These were amusing excursions, where a merry party of pleasant officers from a frontier post, and their guests, a jolly crowd of merchants, brokers, and railroad men from the East, started out to have a buffalo-hunt. With them went the post guide and a scout or two, an escort of soldiers, and the great blue army-wagons, under whose white tilts were piled all the comforts that the post could furnish—unlimited food and drink, and many sacks of forage for the animals. Here all was mirth and jest and good-fellowship, and, except that canvas covered them while they slept, the hunters lived in as much comfort as when at home. The killing of buffalo was to them only an excuse for their jolly outing amid novel scenes.

It was on the plains of Montana, in the days when buffalo were still abundant, that I had one of my last buffalo-hunts—a hunt with a serious purpose. A company of fifty or more men, who for weeks had been living on bacon and beans, longed for the "boss ribs" of fat cow, and when we struck the buffalo range two of us were deputed to kill some meat. My companion was an old prairie-man of great experience, and I myself was not altogether new to the West, for I had hunted in many territories, and had more than once been "jumped" by hostile Indians. Our horses were not buffalo-runners, yet we felt a certain confidence that if we could find a bunch and get a good start on them, we would bring in the desired meat. The troops would march during the day, for the commanding officer had no notion of waiting in camp merely for fresh meat, and we were to go out, hunt, and overtake the command at their night's camp.

The next day after we had reached the buffalo range, we started out long before the eastern sky was gray, and were soon riding off over the chilly prairie. The trail which the command was to follow ran a little north of east, and we kept to the south and away from it, believing that in this direction we would find the game, and that if we started them they would run north or northwest—against the wind, so that we could kill them near the trail. Until some time after the sun had risen, we saw nothing larger than antelope; but at length, from the top of a high hill, we could see, far away to the east, dark dots on the prairie, which we knew could only be buffalo. They were undisturbed too; for, though we watched them for some time, we could detect no motion in their ranks.

It took us nearly two hours to reach the low, broken buttes on the north side of which the buffalo were; and, riding up on the easternmost of these, we tried to locate our game more exactly. It was important to get as close as possible before starting them, so that our first rush might carry us into the midst of them. Knowing the capabilities of our horses, which were thin from long travel, we felt sure that if the buffalo should take the alarm before we were close to them, we could not overtake the cows and young animals, which always run in the van, and should have to content ourselves with old bulls. On the other hand, if we could dash in among them during the first few hundred yards of the race, we should be able to keep up with and select the fattest animals in the herd.

When we reached a point just below the crest of the hill, I stopped and waited, while my companion rode on. Just before he got to the top he too halted, then took off his hat and peered over the ridge, examining so much of the prairie beyond as was now visible to him. His inspection was careful and thorough, and when he had made sure that nothing was in sight, his horse took a step or two forward and then stopped again, and the rider scanned every foot of country before him. The horse, trained as the real hunter's horse is always trained, understood what was required of him, and with pricked ears examined the prairie beyond with as much interest as did his rider. When the calf of Charley's right leg pressed the horse's side, two or three steps more were taken, and then a lifting of the bridle-hand caused another halt.

At length I saw my companion slowly bend forward over his horse's neck, turn, and ride back to me. He had seen the backs of two buffalo lying on the edge of a little flat hardly a quarter of a mile from where we stood. The others of the band must be still nearer to us. By riding along the lowest part of the sag which separated the two buttes, and then down a little ravine, it seemed probable that we could come within a few yards of the buffalo unobserved. Our preparations did not take long. The saddle cinches were loosened, blankets arranged, saddles put in their proper places and tightly cinched again. Cartridges were brought round to the front and right of the belt, where they would be convenient for reloading. Our coats, tied behind the saddle, were looked to, the strings which held them being tightened and securely retied. All this was not lost on our horses, which understood as well as we did what was coming. We skirted the butte, rode through the low sag and down into the little ravine, which soon grew deeper, so that our heads were below the range of vision of almost anything on the butte. Passing the mouth of the little side ravine, however, there came into full view a huge bull, lying well up on the hillside. Luckily his back was toward us, and, each bending low over his horse's neck, we rode on, and in a moment were hidden by the side of the ravine. Two or three minutes more, and we came to another side ravine, which was wide and commanded a view of the flat. We stopped before reaching this, and a peep showed that we were within a few yards of two old cows, a young heifer, and a yearling, all of them to the north of us. Beyond, we could see the backs of others, all lying down.

We jumped on our horses again, and setting the spurs well in, galloped up the ravine and up on the flat; and as we came into view, the nearest buffalo, as if propelled by a huge spring, were on their feet, and, with a second's pause to look, dashed away to the north. Scattered over the flat were fifty or seventy-five buffalo, all of which, by the time we had glanced over the field, were off, with heads bending low to the ground, and short, spiky tails stretched out behind. We were up even with the last of the cows, and our horses were running easily and seemed to have plenty of reserve power. Charley, who was a little ahead of me, called back: "They will cross the trail about a mile north of here. Kill a couple when we get to it." I nodded, and we went on. The herd raced forward over the rolling hills, and in what seemed a very short time we rushed down a long slope on to a wide flat, in which was a prairie-dog town of considerable extent. We were on the very heels of the herd, and in a cloud of dust kicked up by their rapid flight. To see the ground ahead was impossible. We could only trust to our horses and our good luck to save us from falling. Our animals were doing better than we had supposed they could, and were going well and under a pull. I felt that a touch of the spurs and a little riding would bring us up even with the leaders of the buffalo. The pace had already proved too much for several bulls, which had turned off to one side and been passed by. As we flew across the flat, I saw far off a dark line and two white objects, which I knew must be our command. I called to my comrade, and, questioning by the sign, pointed at the buffalo. He nodded, and in a moment we had given free rein to our horses and were up among the herd. During the ride I had two or three times selected my game, but the individuals of the band changed positions so constantly that I could not keep track of them. Now, however, I picked out a fat two-year-old bull; but as I drew up to him he ran faster than before, and rapidly made his way toward the head of the band. I was resolved that he should not escape, and so, though I was still fifteen or twenty yards in the rear, fired. At the shot he fell heels over head directly across a cow which was running by his side and a little behind him. I saw her turn a somersault, and almost at the same instant heard Charley shoot twice in quick succession, and saw two buffalo fall. I fired at a fat young cow that I had pushed my pony up close to. At the shot she whirled, my horse did the same, and she chased me as hard as she could go for seventy-five yards, while I did some exceedingly vigorous spurring, for she was close behind me all the time. To do my horse justice, I think that he would have run as fast as he could, even without the spurs, for he appreciated the situation. At no time was there any immediate danger that the cow would overtake us; if there had been, I should have dodged her. Presently the cow stopped, and stood there very sick. When I rode back, I did not find it easy to get my horse near her; but another shot was not needed, and while I sat looking at her she fell over dead. The three buffalo first killed had fallen within a hundred yards of the trail where the wagons afterward passed, and my cow was but little farther away. The command soon came up, the soldiers did the butchering, and before long we were on the march again across the parched plain.

Of the millions of buffalo which even in our own time ranged the plains in freedom, none now remain. From the prairies which they used to darken, the wild herds, down to the last straggling bull, have disappeared. In the Yellowstone National Park, protected from destruction by United States troops, are the only wild buffalo which exist within the borders of the United States. These are mountain buffalo, and, from their habit of living in the thick timber and on the rough mountain-sides, they are only now and then seen by visitors to the park. It is impossible to say just how many there are, but from the best information that I can get, based on the estimates of reliable and conservative men, I conclude that the number was not less than four hundred in the winter of 1891-92. Each winter or spring the government scout employed in the park sees one or more herds of these buffalo, and as such herds are usually made up in part of young animals and have calves with them, it is fair to assume that they are steadily, if slowly, increasing. The report of a trip made in January, 1892, speaks of four herds seen in the Hayden Valley, which numbered respectively 78, 50, 110, and 15. Besides these, a number of scattering groups were seen at a distance, which would bring the number up to three hundred.

In the far northwest, in the Peace River district, there may still be found a few wood buffalo. They are seldom killed, and the estimate of their numbers varies from five hundred to fifteen hundred. This cannot be other than the merest guess, since they are scattered over many thousand square miles of territory which is without inhabitants, and for the most part unexplored.

On the great plains is still found the buffalo skull half buried in the soil and crumbling to decay. The deep trails once trodden by the marching hosts are grass-grown now, and fast filling up. When these most enduring relics of a vanished race shall have passed away, there will be found, in all the limitless domain once darkened by their feeding herds, not one trace of the American buffalo.

George Bird Grinnell.

Nights with the Grizzlies

In this paper I propose to give an account of some experience with the grizzly bear in the summer and fall of 1885. Here let me correct some impressions prevailing among sportsmen from the East as to the proper time to hunt this animal. As detailed in the sporting papers, one sportsman hunting late in the fall finds them at the timber-line, and having some success and basing his opinion upon statements of his guide, is satisfied that is the only place to find them, and that you must stealthily follow the trail through dense timber, as he did. Another sportsman finds them below the foot-hills among the Bad Lands, and thinks that is the proper locality; and so each one is governed by his own particular good luck and experience. This reminds me of the heated controversy that agitated some of the readers of one of the sporting papers a few years since as to the color of the jack-rabbit of the plains: one party contending they were gray and the opposing party that they were white, each party citing his own restricted experience with that fleet-footed animal. To those having more extended observation it was plain that each side was to a certain extent right as well as wrong, for it is well known that the jack-rabbit is gray during summer and fall and turns white in the winter, and then again sheds his white coat in spring: at least this is the case in Wyoming and Montana.

So with the grizzly. He is essentially an omnivorous animal: his food varying with each season and the locality where such food is obtained, his habitat varies accordingly. He lies in his winter bed until routed out by the melting of the winter snow, and the ground being still frozen, he has to rustle for his grub. He soon becomes poor from the necessity of much traveling around for old carcasses and whatever food comes handy. He is then usually in the foot-hills. In the summer his food is more vegetable—grass, roots, plants, etc. His haunt is then on the highest mountain plateaus, where he does a great deal of rooting in a certain kind of loose rock and loam. In the last of summer, berries are ripe, and he is then found below the foot-hills, and in the Bad Lands, or wherever chokeberries, plums, bulberries, etc., are found. In the fall he craves animal food, and is then found high up in the foot-hills, or again on the mountain plateaus, wherever game is most abundant; and in November and December he seeks his winter quarters. These remarks do not apply to grizzly bears that are found in the Bad Lands bordering the Missouri or the Lower Yellowstone, as they live there the entire year, "holing up" in winter in the bluffs of those desolate-looking regions.

The intellect and intelligence of the grizzly bear are not fully appreciated. Strip him of his hide, stand him erect on his hind feet, stick a plug hat on his upper end, and he resembles in anatomy and general appearance that "noblest work of God"—man: a little too long-bodied, neck a little short, but otherwise, looking at the muscles of his thighs and forearm, a veritable athlete. Re-clothe him in his fur, place him on his all fours, watch him rooting around for grubs and worms and carrion, and wallowing in mud and filth, and he resembles in apparent stupidity and habits the lowest type of animal—the hog. Yet those well acquainted with his characteristics will, I think, agree with me that in intelligence and perhaps even in intellect he is not many grades in the process of evolution below man.

**Prospecting for Grub.
From Scribner's Magazine.**

About the middle of July, 1885, word reached me that there was considerable sign of bear "rooting" on some high mountain plateaus not many days' travel by pack-train from my ranch. Taking a pack outfit, including my fur-lined sleeping-bag, a good mountain man, and a lad of fifteen to take care of camp and the horses, and enough grub for a few days, we reached the locality, after a hard climb, about noon on the 18th of July. We made camp at about 8,500 feet elevation on the head of one of the forks of Four Bear Creek, having to pack wood up from below for making coffee.

We struck out after lunch up the gulch, and after going a few miles discovered a grizzly rooting among the rocks well up to its head, near the summit of the range, which is here between 10,000 and 11,000 feet elevation. A reconnaissance indicated that the only chance to approach him to windward was by crossing the mountain to the right into the valley of another fork of Four Bear Creek. Accordingly, we climbed over the mountain divide and were making along its opposite slope, when just in our front about a mile off, near the head of the gulch on the right, was discovered another grizzly rooting. It was agreed that I was to have the shot, and it became necessary to leave my horse and dogs back with the men. I took it afoot. A little study of the ground showed that in order to approach him successfully, it was necessary to descend to the bottom of the gorge on the right, and to ascend along its bed. This I proceeded to do. Just before reaching the bed of the gorge I was exposed to view, and was walking fast or running to get the advantage of its friendly cover. When within about fifty yards of the bottom, and with my attention directed to the bear about half a mile away, a large grizzly forced himself on my attention by rising from his bed in the bottom of the gulch. Walking slowly away, he commenced ascending diagonally the opposite and steep side of the gorge. The old rascal during the heat of the day had dug a resting-place in the cool bed of the branch, was taking his siesta, and evidently resented being disturbed. From the sullen way in which he made off, occasionally looking back, I felt he was going to be ugly. Quicker than it takes to write it, I had two cartridges in my right hand, which, with the one in the rifle, were thought sufficient, for at that time the size of the beast was not realized. The cartridge in the rifle was a 110-270-grain express, and those in the hand 110-270-grain and 110-340-grain respectively, all express-balls.

While making these preparations, the bear, going diagonally up the side of the gulch, had disappeared behind a huge conglomerate boulder that overhung the stream. Seeing he must soon emerge, I dropped on my right knee and stood ready to fire at the first favorable opportunity. In a moment he emerged from behind the boulder, walked up a short distance, stopped and looked back, exposing his left side to rather more than a quartering shot. Aim was quickly taken for his heart. A report followed, and the little express-ball did its work well. It broke two ribs, three or four large fragments entered the heart, and the balance of the splinters scattered through the lungs. Making but little noise when hit,—an ugly sigh,—he, as this species of bear almost always does under like circumstances, tucked his head between his hind legs, and rolled down into the gulch, using his fore legs for guides. He came up with a bounce, was on his feet in a moment and making a rush straight for me. I had loaded in a jiffy with the other 110-270-grain cartridge, but waited a moment until he commenced ascending my side of the gulch, hoping with a good shot to roll him back. Crossing rapidly the bed of the gulch, he was in a moment ascending toward me, and when within about thirty yards (he was originally about seventy yards at the first fire) I fired at his front, hitting at the point of the right shoulder, shattering the socket-joint and that bone half-way to the elbow. He did not roll back, but was demoralized and sickened, and had not the sand to come further, but changing his direction to the left about forty-five degrees, passed within twenty yards of my right front. I was loaded and ready for another shot as he passed. He appeared so near done for, however, that I hesitated to fire, wishing to have some practice on him for my two young dogs Bob and Snip, which had never seen a live bear. He, however, seemed, after passing, to mend his licks so fast that I feared he would give trouble in despatching him, so I ran rapidly after him, he in the mean time having partially disappeared under the bank; and when within fifteen or twenty yards he turned at bay, facing me. Before he could charge, if such was his aim, the 110-340-grain cartridge was delivered into the side of the neck within the collar-bone, making a fearful wound, and rolling him down into the gulch, where he soon died. It was only after my man had come up and the bear had been rolled over that his dimensions and the danger I escaped by the little ball doing such execution at the socket-joint were realized. Had it struck an inch and a half to the left, he would have been on me in a few more jumps; and though another shot would have been given, I think, unless it had been a paralyzing shot in the brain or spinal column, he could have so torn and lacerated me as to make death preferable.

I have been in half a dozen scrapes of more or less danger with these bears, but have never lost my presence of mind until they were dead, and the danger passed through realized. I have always determined never to run, but to face them and fire away, believing that the least sign of fear gives any animal additional courage.

I had an adventure similar to this with, a she-bear that had been approached within fifty-seven yards. It was a bright moonlight night, and her cub was squalling in a beaver-trap by her side. A good shot was delivered over the heart. Three shots were discharged as she rushed forward, first by myself, then one from Le Corey, who was backing me, and then another by myself; and when the "racket" was over, the bear was lying dead twelve yards from us. All these shots were bull's-eyes and deadly. In this case I could not have run had the spirit moved me, as from a serious accident I had been on crutches or my back for twenty-four days, and hobbled up the mountain in this instance with the help of a crutch and a stick, Le carrying my rifle.

A familiarity with all the breech-actions of the day, together with an extended experience with the Sharps system, has convinced me that the latter system, in safety, facility, and rapidity of manipulation, is not equaled by any. Take the next best, the double-barreled rifle: only two shots could have been delivered in the two before-described adventures. I have never had sufficient confidence in any of the repeating rifles to use them against dangerous game, when so much better could be had. Their want of power, their facility for getting out of order at the wrong time, especially when rapidly manipulated, combined with the fact that their rapidity of fire is very little greater than a system like the Sharps, are the considerations that have influenced me. In my opinion there has not yet been invented a repeating apparatus that is equal, under all circumstances, to the human hands in connection with a good breech system.

A better idea of these bears can be had from measurements than from weight. The bear first alluded to was a very large one (one among three of the largest ever killed by me), and, judging by one killed and weighed subsequently, he probably weighed 600 pounds, though not fat. His length, as he would have stood, was 6 feet 10 inches. Measurements show that he could have stood erect on his hind feet to the height of 8 feet. His head was 18 inches long by 12 inches wide; his hind foot 11-1/2 inches by 6 inches; fore foot, without the toes, 7 by 6 inches. His forearm, after being skinned, measured 18 inches around; his skull, which is preserved, 15-7/8 inches by 9 inches. The tusks projected from the gums 1-5/8 inches.

With the 45-caliber rifle used, I have killed nearly 40 bears—all, with the exception of this one, with a 340-grain express-ball. This 270-grain express bullet was a 44-caliber used for several years on deer from a 44-caliber rifle. It did very good work in this instance, but for a large bear the heavier ball is preferable. The 270-grain ball flies remarkably true for its weight.

In the process of skinning the bear, it was found that this was not the first encounter he had had with mankind. In the muscles of the neck, and of the right fore leg above the elbow and next to the bone, were found four rifle-balls, and a large fragment of another ball. The wounds had healed up, and each ball was inclosed in a sac with the appearance of having been there several years: one 42-caliber 205-grain lead ball lay in the muscles of the neck, another of same caliber and weight, two 50-caliber 375-grain lead balls, and the large flattened fragment of a ball were in the muscles of one fore leg next to the bone. The 42-caliber balls I judged were fired from a '66 model, 44-caliber Winchester, and as all the balls were little battered and did not shatter the bone, they must have been fired from a rim-fire cartridge; all the balls were cannelured.

The bear I was after when this one was stumbled on, took to his heels and disappeared rapidly over the mountain after the second shot. We went for the first one seen, but the dogs getting the wind of him, and having a taste of bear's blood, ignominiously "broke" and stirred him up. We chased him on horseback and afoot for three quarters of a mile, but did not get near enough to get in an effectual shot. The dogs, that had never before chased a live bear, could run alongside of him, but did not take hold. Probably you or I would have done the same thing under the circumstances.

Haying-time cut short this hunt. A short time afterward one of my neighbors complained of the depredations of bears among his thoroughbred cattle, having recently lost two yearlings. I suggested that if he would furnish the medicine in the shape of a carcass, a repetition of such business might be stopped. He agreed, and I at once reconnoitered the locality and selected a point in the valley of a small mountain stream, where he promptly had the carcass planted. An almost daily inspection was made of the medicine, but not until the morning of the seventh day were there any indications of its being disturbed. Promptly on hand at five o'clock that evening, I was rather incautiously approaching under cover of a slight rise of ground and the sage-brush, and had gotten within 150 yards, when a dark object that to my startled imagination appeared ten feet high, and proportionately broad, appeared to rise out of the earth. Recognizing the situation at once, I rose up offhand and pulled, but the firing-pin failed. This had never before happened under such circumstances, and only half a dozen times in the rifle's history, for want of attention to the firing-bolt. The bear gave me time to cock and fire, but as no answering "bawl" came, the shot was evidently a miss, resulting from my being "put out" by the previous mishap. He was rapidly followed to the edge of the willow swamp (about 150 yards), through which the trail passed, where he was seen, evidently unwilling to forego his evening meal. He quickly sat up, made me out, and at once disappeared before a shot could be delivered. I gave him up for the time, very much discouraged at failing to bag such a large grizzly. He was evidently a boar, and certainly was not much scared, and from his size and actions I was satisfied he was the one that had stolen my neighbor's yearlings. The next evening, August 17, I was on hand early; but, acting on previous experience, took a different position on his trail a hundred yards from the medicine. The direction of the wind forced me to take position with my back to the brush from which the bear would probably appear. This did not suit me. On first arriving on the ground, a dark object came rapidly down the mountain-side, about one mile up the valley, through an opening. This evidently was a bear, though not apparently as large as my friend of the evening before; and I felt sure he would make his appearance did he not take the alarm. Lying down, protected by some sage-brush, I waited patiently until the gray dusk of approaching twilight, but no bear appeared on the scene.

Can you recall your feelings when, as a boy, you passed through a graveyard at the hour of dusk, thinking, with the poet,

'T is now the very witching time of night,When churchyards yawn,
and hell itself breathes outContagion to this world?

With what superstitious dread you looked cautiously around, expecting a hobgoblin at any moment to rise out of the ground? How every noise—the crackling of a twig—startled you? So it is with me when watching on the trail of this bear at such an hour. When occasion requires it, his movement is as stealthy and noiseless as a cat's. You hear the rolling of a boulder up the mountain-side in the timber several hundred yards away. You know it must be done by some large animal, and you suspect a bear. Presently the same noise, but closer, and your faculties are all on the *qui vive*, and you are every moment expecting his appearance. You wait what, to the excited senses, appears a long time. What has become of him? It was, perhaps, a false alarm, and you are discouraged; when, presently, there he stands, apparently right on you, and seemingly risen out of the ground.

So it was on this occasion, as I lay in the open about thirty feet from the thicket, in a prone position in the grass, clothed in soiled buckskin, with three cartridges in left hand and finger on trigger, ready to rise into a sitting position and deliver fire. Hark! the crackling of brush almost behind me. It is a moment of intense interest, for I don't know where he will appear. My attention is kept constantly to the rear and left rear. No more noise. What has become of him? It is getting very dark, and maybe it was a mistake. Presently, there! right on me apparently, but really fifty yards to the left rear, stands a black mass that must be the bear. I rise cautiously to a sitting position, and as he stands, looking wistfully up toward the old horse, I pull away at his side. The report is followed by a suppressed bawl, and he rolls over. I am loaded in a moment and waiting to see if he regains his feet. He does not, and it is unnecessary to fire. I walk up to him with finger on trigger at a ready, but the death-rattle is in his throat, and another shot is unnecessary. He turns out to be a black bear with a very black coat, and pretty well furred. He is dressed as quickly as possible, for it is now dark, and quite six miles to quarters, over a trailless mountain. A walk of half a mile to my horse Pike, and then as rapid a ride home as circumstances will admit, wind up the evening's adventures. I am well satisfied, but know I have not yet gotten the right one, the "calf-killer."

Rush skins and attends to the hide the next morning, and before sundown I am again on hand. The old horse is fast disappearing, and it is desirable to lose no time. Position is taken this time a little nearer the trail. In coming out from the willow-brush it passes for twenty or thirty yards through a marsh that is screened, to some extent, by scattering willows on the near side; and my position enables me to see, through these willows, a portion of the trail over which the bear will probably come. Late in the afternoon a storm had passed around the mountain, and a strong and favorable wind was blowing. Lying prone among the sage-brush, in a position favorable for observation, with everything at a ready, I wait patiently. Sundown comes; the mountain to the west casts its shadows around. It becomes quite dusky: so much so that I experiment as to whether the fore sight can be seen, otherwise a wad of white paper must be tied over the front sight. This is as yet unnecessary. It is now the witching time when this bear likes to prowl around. The senses are all on the strain as they are directed to the left rear. Just then a dark moving mass flits by between the willows on the trail, and soon emerges in full view, but again to disappear in a slight depression passed by the trail. Heavens, what a monster he seems in the dim twilight! As soon as he disappears I move rapidly and noiselessly forward to within about fifty yards of the trail he has to pass, drop on the right knee, and am ready. He does not come to time, however, and has evidently stopped to listen; doubtless remembering the first evening's experience, and being in hearing of last evening's racket. Has he taken the alarm and gone back? When on the point of going to the left, peering over, and taking a chance shot on the run, his back appears over the sage-brush and he is moving confidently forward, having satisfied himself there is no danger. At the first favorable opportunity, as he passes through the sage-brush, I deliver fire into his side, a little too high, and he rolls over, but with such a bawl as to indicate he is dangerous, did he know from what direction came the shot. He is soon on his feet, going back on his trail, toward the swamp. Loading quickly, I run forward to intercept him, and find him, after stumbling along 40 or 50 yards, in a sitting position near the edge of the marsh, evidently nearly done for, with his back toward me. A moment's interval was sufficient to place a ball in the back of his head; he rolls over, and is soon dead. A hasty examination showed him to be a large bear, and the handsomest and most symmetrically formed I had ever killed. He was in just the proper flesh for activity and business, though not quite as large as the big bear killed on the Big Bear Fork of Four Bear Creek, heretofore described.

Before proceeding to disembowel him, I did what had always been done under like circumstances—that is, placed the loaded rifle convenient for instant use. Something whispered this caution, especially now, as it was a time when another bear might appear on the trail at any moment. Keeping my eyes as much as possible at the point on the opposite side of the marsh, where the trail debouched on to it, I had proceeded to rip the carcass from the throat to the pelvis, and had my hands already messed up in a mass of liver, paunch, express-balls, etc., etc., when my attention was drawn to a dark mass at that point, and in a moment my rifle was in hand ready for the emergency. By the time I was ready to fire he had discovered something unusual in his front, and had "sat up" to make me out. Before doing so, aim had been quickly taken at his brisket, and at the report he had tumbled over, the ball striking the left side, fragments penetrating the heart. Judging from his boldness in stumbling on to me, not more than fifteen minutes after my last shot, I expected that he would show fight, but instead he made back on his trail as fast as his condition would allow. From previous experience in just such circumstances, the necessity was at once recognized of a cautious but vigorous pursuit, if he was to be secured before hiding in the brush; and without hesitation I plunged through the marsh, half knee-deep in mud and water, and entered the narrow trail on the opposite side. Pursuing it rapidly for thirty or forty yards to where it passed through a little opening, there, within ten steps of me, was a dark mass, breathing heavily and lying partially behind a small clump of willows. Putting a telling shot through the center of the mass, he appeared to wake up, and gave an exhibition of some of the grandest ground and lofty tumbling, at one time appearing to stand up on his head and kicking with his hind feet ten feet straight into the air. As he did not get upon his feet again, another shot was unnecessary, and he soon settled down and was dead.

This bear was as large from tip to tip as he of the Big Bear Fork, but not as fat nor as large-bodied; in fact, not as heavy as the one just killed. Neither of these bears, I think, needed a second shot, and, undisturbed, would not have gotten on their feet again. A dense thicket was near, and they might have scrambled into its cover and have been lost, so another shot was given. At any rate, darkness was at hand by the time the carcasses were dressed, and a dense fog was settling over the mountain that had to be crossed. The exhilaration of spirits from the killing of two such large bears on the same evening—one of them the bear that I was after—caused me to forget fatigue and fog, and with a light heart Pike was mounted and the mountain ascended. A thick fog soon enveloped us, so that nothing could be seen beyond a hundred feet. Pike and I soon disagreed as to the direction, but I insisted on my way. After going a half-mile and getting into some rough ground, it was evident that I was wrong and completely befogged. The rein was then given to Pike, and he turned squarely to the left, and, having gone 600 yards over some pretty rough ground, he came to the head of the game-trail leading down the mountain, and which we had several times traveled. Pike had his way the balance of the ride, and after passing across the drainage for two miles we got below the fog, and by ten o'clock we were once more at home.

As an indication of the labor usually undergone in hunting this bear, it is stated that seventy-five miles were traveled (one half of which was in the night) before the first shot, and one hundred and five miles before killing the three. I have since traveled more than a hundred miles after a special bear and was repaid by only one shot at long range, and no bear.

The next day Rush and McDevitt skinned and packed in the hides and fat of the two grizzlies. The weighing apparatus was taken along, and the "calf-killer" was found to weigh 405 pounds after being dressed sixteen hours, the other something less. The black bear was not weighed, but it is presumed he weighed about the average of this species (175 pounds) in life.

The rifle employed is the same used for several years, a 45-caliber Sharps, with which I have killed thirty-eight of these bears, of which number twenty-two were killed with a single shot each, using 110 grains C. & H. No. 6, and a 340-grain express-ball. As I have before stated, the rise of its trajectory is 7.01 inches in 200 yards, an average of about twenty shots through a trajectory range. Previously I had used a 44-caliber Sharps, with a bottle-neck shell holding 100 to 105 grains of the same powder with which a good many bears had been killed. No especial ball has been determined on as best for bear and elk and sheep. With exceptional opportunities for several years past among all our big game, together with a careful study of the subject, based on a dissection of wounds made by different combinations of powder and ball, I think the 2-7/8 45-caliber shell, with 110 grains strong powder and a 340-grain express-ball such as I use, the most destructive charge in all American rifles for bear, elk, and sheep. A little lighter ball might answer, perhaps, but I am not sure. The amount of powder would not be sufficient for a heavier one for best results. The best results not only depend on the relative proportion of powder and ball, but also on the diameter and depth of the hole in the point of ball. If the walls around the hole are too thin, they will break off too soon, or in too fine pieces. If the walls are too thick, they may not disintegrate until the ball's velocity has been so much retarded that the particles will not have velocity to make their own way, but will follow the channel made by the butt; so that a good many considerations enter into the problem. The ball in question, shot directly into a bear, elk, sheep, etc., will, after passing through the skin, break up, usually tearing a hole through the ribs, even of a fat animal, through which the unclenched hand can be passed, the fragments scattering in a cone shape, the larger fragments penetrating to the opposite ribs. In this way the whole momentum of the ball is expended on the vitals, the heart and lungs. Hit further back it breaks up into still smaller fragments, making a terrible wound in the paunch and entrails that none of those animals can long survive. I have never known it to fail in breaking the large bones of the largest bear or elk when coming in contact with them.

For deer and antelope my 40-caliber is found sufficient, using 100 grains of strong powder and a particular express-ball of 270 grains. It makes about a 6-1/2-inch curve in two hundred yards, and the ball flies very true. I use also in the 45-caliber the 44-caliber ball before alluded to, using three thicknesses of patch paper. It flies remarkably true for its weight, and makes a 6.34-inch curve per 200 yards, with 110 grains C. & H. No. 6. I failed to say at the proper place that the degree of hardness or per cent. of alloy has a great deal to do with the execution, as well as accuracy of flight, of the express-ball. When of pure lead they break up too soon. Nor have I ever known a reasonable degree of accuracy obtained with any lead ball with a comparatively large charge, beyond 50 or 75 yards. They are knocked out of proper shape by the time they leave the muzzle. This want of accuracy has been observed with the best English express-rifles with light leaden balls. I find in my experience with the balls of my preference (as above) that from five per cent. for the heavier ball, to eight per cent. for the lighter, is best.

A 20-bore double-barreled shot-gun, made by Bland & Sons, of London (chambered for the Kynoch brass shell), for ducks, the several species of grouse, jack-rabbits, magpies, skunks, etc., completes my battery. I value the latter very highly for its "executive ability," combined with a weight of only six pounds.

I have written much in detail, because I think it is the details that make the account of hunting trips interesting. I hope its perusal may interest readers as much as the recalling of its incidents has interested me.

I have made several mentions of Four Bear Creek. The name was given it for want of a better one by the United States Land Surveyors, who happened to be in camp on Hell-Roaring River, near the creek's mouth, on the night in which I killed four bears, the last about 9.30 o'clock at night.

W. D. Pickett.

The Yellowstone Park as a Game Reservation

When the Yellowstone Park was set aside by Act of Congress as a national reservation, very little was known of the region beyond such facts as could be gathered during one short season of exploration, mainly devoted to an examination of the marvelous hot springs and geysers, which have since made the place so famous throughout the world.

During his first visit to the region in 1871, Dr. F. V. Hayden realized the exceptional nature of the hydrothermal manifestations found here and the grand scale upon which the phenomena were displayed. Although it was then far removed from all beaten tracks, he shrewdly foresaw the necessity of government protection, if these scientific curiosities were to be preserved intact in their natural condition. He saw that vandals would soon despoil the region of the delicate incrustations and sediments slowly deposited through long ages from thermal waters, and that settlers, learning their real value, would seize upon all objects of interest for their own gain.

**The Buffalo of the Timber.
Photographed from life by John Fossam. From Forest and Stream.**

On his return to Washington he urged the enactment of a law establishing the Yellowstone Park as a government reservation. In this work he was ably supported by Senators Anthony, of Rhode Island, Edmunds, of Vermont, and Trumbull, of Illinois, and also by Mr. Dawes, of Massachusetts, then a member of the House of

Representatives, who in an excellent speech presented the matter so forcibly that the enabling act passed the House without opposition.

The report of the Public Lands Committee of the House recommending the passage of the act, after pointing out the worthlessness of the region for agricultural purposes or for settlement, closes with this expression of opinion, valuable in the light in which the Park is now held by the civilized world:

The withdrawal of this tract, therefore, from sale or settlement takes nothing from the value of the public domain, and is no pecuniary loss to the Government, but will be regarded by the entire civilized world as a step of progress and an honor to Congress and the nation.

The organic law establishing the Park, after defining its boundaries, states that the reservation is "dedicated and set apart as a public park or pleasure-ground for the benefit and enjoyment of the people." Exclusive control of the Park was given to the Secretary of the Interior, with power to make the necessary rules and regulations for its proper care and maintenance. He was authorized to "provide against the wanton destruction of the fish and game found within said Park, and against their capture or destruction for the purpose of merchandise or profit." The act was approved by the President March 1, 1872.

It will thus be seen that from the very inception of the project for a grand National Park, the preservation of the game was contemplated, although it is evident that absolute prohibition of shooting was not then intended. Probably this was not deemed necessary in such a remote and unfrequented region, to say nothing of its working a hardship upon those who were ready to penetrate its forests and search for fresh wonders.

At that time the country included within the Park was practically an inaccessible region, which, owing to the rough and rugged nature of its barriers, had defied all earlier attempts at exploration. It stood out alone as a broad unknown mountain mass when the surrounding country had been fairly well explored. It had been visited only by a few venturesome pioneers, mining prospectors, and fur-hunters, who found little or no encouragement to seekers after wealth. Only one trans-continental railway spanned the Rocky Mountains, crossing Wyoming far to the south of the Park, the Union and Central Pacific having been opened to traffic in 1869. At that time, wild animals roamed freely over prairie, plain, and mountain slope, from the Canadian border to the Rio Grande. In Montana, Wyoming, and Colorado, elk, deer, and antelope abounded in favorable localities. In the North Park in northern Colorado, I saw almost daily numerous bands of antelope, hundreds in each, grazing along the shallow bottom-lands. Over the Laramie plains, antelope and deer might be seen almost any day from the railway. Buffalo roamed the great plains in vast numbers. In 1872 I saw buffalo in the North Park, but they long since left that ideal grazing-ground. The Upper Missouri and Yellowstone valleys were the homes of magnificent herds; now they have disappeared forever. I never had the good fortune to see such enormous herds as frequently wandered over western Kansas; but I well remember one autumn afternoon, when seated in a railway car, book in hand, glancing out upon the prairie, as I turned the pages, I scarcely looked up from the volume but the shaggy forms of buffalo were visible; and this continued until darkness cut off the view. To-day none are to be seen. Except under protection, buffalo have practically become extinct. Elk, moose, deer, antelope, and mountain sheep are gradually retiring to more and more secluded mountain recesses. Year by year game areas become more restricted, even in the mountain regions. The lumberman and railway-tie cutter, the advance-guard of a constantly increasing civilization, are steadily encroaching upon the haunts of game.

Large areas of the Rocky Mountain country are timberless and in great part waterless during portions of the year. In such sections the bare rocks carry very little soil and afford an insufficient food-supply for game. In many instances where the natural conditions would otherwise be favorable, the mountains rise as long narrow ridges between relatively broad valleys. On the occupation of the lowlands by a steadily increasing population, such game-resorts became easily accessible to butchers and skin-hunters. The game was either soon killed off, or the instinct of self-preservation taught the animals to abandon their haunts for more secluded pastures. No better instance of the quickness with which animals perceive danger need be mentioned than their migration from the Big Horn Mountains, when that once admirable game-country was suddenly invaded by hunters from all parts of the world. It is true that the game was slaughtered in vast numbers, but it is equally true that the animals migrated to less disturbed regions. For years the Big Horn Mountains have been known as a gameless country; "shot out" was the expressive phrase applied to them by hide and horn hunters. The urgent necessity for game-preservation, if it is desired to protect our larger animals from extermination, is apparent.

At the time the Yellowstone Park was set aside, the country was almost a *terra incognita*; its boundaries were ill defined. Since then it has become famous throughout the world, and is annually visited by thousands of people, attracted there by many scientific and scenic features. Gradually its importance became known, both as a national forest reservation and as a natural storage reservoir, which, if properly protected, will supply through broad rivers the arid regions below with much-needed waters. Its fitness for a grand national game reservation soon became manifest to a few people familiar with the far West, and with the disappearance elsewhere of our large Rocky Mountain animals. The necessity for rules against the shooting of any and all animals was early recognized, and for several years such rules have been strictly enforced with beneficial results.

In recent years, with a better understanding of the country, its timber, water supply, the picturesqueness of its scenery, and its natural advantages for game, an effort has been made to enlarge the reservation on the south and east and to clearly mark its boundaries. By this proposed enlargement, the sources of the Yellowstone and Snake rivers, and the greater part of the Absaroka Range on the east, would be included within the Park. It is believed that this additional territory will before long be made a part of the Park reservation by the action of Congress, as it has already been set aside as a timber reservation and placed in charge of the superintendent of the Park. In speaking, therefore, of the superior advantages of the region as a home for animals, the timber reservation will be meant as well as the Park itself.

The area of the Yellowstone Park, as at present defined, is somewhat more than 3300 square miles. The central portion is a broad volcanic plateau between 7000 and 8500 feet above sea-level, with an average elevation of 8000 feet. Surrounding it on the south, east, north, and northwest, lying partly within and partly without the Park lines, are mountain-ranges with culminating peaks and ridges rising from 2000 to 4000 feet above the general level of the inclosed table-land. Beyond the mountains the country falls away on all sides, the lowlands and valleys varying in altitude from 4000 to 6000 feet. The entire region stands out as a bold mountain mass, measuring approximately 75 miles in width by 60 miles in length, which rises high above the adjoining country.

Although it is commonly so called, the central portion of this mass is not, strictly speaking, a plateau; at least it is by no means a level region, but an undulating country, broken by abrupt escarpments and long table-like ridges of gently inclined rocks. It is accidented by shallow depressions and valleys of varied outline, the irregularities of lava flows adding much to the diversity of surface forms and features. Deep cañons and gorges cut the plateau, and penetrate nearly to the base of the accumulated lavas. These nearly horizontal lavas rest against the steeper slopes of the encircling mountains. The foot-hills, in contrast with the plateau, afford a more broken character, the intermontane valleys become deeper, the country gradually growing rougher until the higher summit of the ranges present an indescribable array of crags and precipices reaching far above the timber-line. The Rocky Mountains nowhere offer a rougher tract of country than the Absaroka Range bordering the Park on the east. Such an elevated mass naturally becomes a storm center, attracting moisture-laden clouds. The concentration and precipitation of this moisture in the form of rain and snow furnishes during the year an amount of water exceptionally large for the Rocky Mountains. An abundant supply of rain and snow favors a forest growth, which in turn aids to conserve the water. In consequence a luxuriant growth of nutritious grasses springs up, accompanied by a varied undergrowth of bush and shrub. Observation of mountain, valley, and plateau shows that about 84 per cent. of the Park is forest-clad. Over the greater part of the timber reservation the proportion of forest is not quite so great, much of the higher mountains being above timber-line, or else in the southern part more open and park-like, with long stretches of grass-lands dotted here and there with groups of picturesque pines.

Across the plateau, with a very sinuous course, stretches the Continental Divide, separating the waters of the Atlantic from those of the Pacific. On the plateau on both sides of this divide lie magnificent sheets of water, notably the Yellowstone, Shoshone, Lewis and Heart lakes, forming a most characteristic feature of the country. This part of the Park has been designated the "lake region." Hundreds of smaller lakes and ponds occupy depressions either in the ancient lava flows or in basins of glacial origin. Scattered over plateau and mountain are bogs, marshes, and meadows in marked contrast to most of the Rocky Mountain country. Innumerable perennial springs reach the surface from beneath the rocks. Around the borders of these lakes and ponds stretch fringes of alpine meadows, affording excellent grazing-grounds. Yellowstone Lake, with a shore-line of nearly 100 miles, is encircled by old lake terraces and glacial benches covered with bunch grass and capable of supporting large herds of wild animals. To one familiar with the plateau along the continental watershed it is possible to travel for miles keeping clear of timber by following from one to the other the open, winding glades and long stretches of meadows and shallow drainage-channels which carry the melting snows to the sources of the Yellowstone and Snake rivers. It is in these secluded nooks and sheltered spots that one finds the game.

A reservation for the protection and maintenance of our large game under natural conditions requires an extensive region unbroken by an area adapted for the abode of man or subject to the disturbances of a continuous traffic. With the rapid encroachments of civilization in the Rocky Mountains, these conditions demand that the country set apart should be unfit for agricultural purposes, and free from mineral resources to tempt the cupidity of the advance-guard of settlers. The Yellowstone Park meets the requirements of such a natural reservation better than any other locality that could be selected. The severity of its climate during the greater part of the year renders the region a forbidding one for settlement and permanent occupation by man. On the other hand, the broad expanse of forest incloses sequestered nooks, and enticing grassy parks, with absolute seclusion in mountain recesses admirably adapted for the homes of wild animals. It is the great diversity of its physical features, offering within a restricted area all the requirements for animal life, which fits it for the home of big game. Abundant food supply, shelter from wind and weather in winter, cool resorts on the uplands in summer, favorable localities for breeding purposes and the rearing of young, all are found here. The Park supplies what is really needed—a zoölogical reservation where big game may roam unmolested by the intrusion of man, rather than a zoölogical garden inclosed by fences, and the game fed or sustained more or less by artificial methods. To most travelers who make the accustomed tour and seldom leave the beaten track, it is a surprise and regret that they see so little game, and they are apt to question its existence in any considerable numbers. In summer the game seldom frequents the geyser basins or places of popular resort, but wanders about undisturbed by the throng of pleasure-seekers. If one wishes to see game he must leave the dusty roads and noisy stages, and travel by pack-train the unfrequented trails into the secluded portions of the Park. Few care to take this trouble, as the rules, rigidly enforced, prevent the trying of their skill with the rifle, when they meet the objects of their search. For game protection scouts, foresters, and gamekeepers are required. These could not well be supplied, except at great expense, were it not that the natural wonders of the region, which each season attracts such large crowds, demand for the maintenance of peace and order that United States troops be stationed there for the protection of the Park, and the observance of the necessary rules and regulations. All the large game animals of the northern Rocky Mountains are known in the Park except the white goat (*Mazama montana*) and the caribou (*Rangifer tarandus*), and it seems probable that the former, if introduced, would remain, as their favorite haunts, mountain fastnesses, are not unlike the Absarokas. Elk, moose, deer, antelope, mountain sheep, buffalo, and bears are found. Of all the game, elk most abound, roaming over mountain, plateau, and valley alike, the higher portions in summer, the lower in winter. For elk, the park is an ideal country. They frequent the alpine meadows and grassy terraces, passing freely from one to the other of the open uplands. Where streams flow through these openings, or ponds occupy shallow depressions, the elk resort to them in large numbers during summer and autumn. The accompanying picture gives an excellent illustration of such a favorite haunt.

In midsummer cows and calves frequent the picturesque park-like country near the sources of the Snake River. In my opinion, the head waters of the Snake furnish one of the best breeding grounds for elk anywhere to be found. In winter they descend to the broad valley-bottoms, where food is accessible and shelter easily obtained. In traveling over the country about these feeders to the Snake, I have been impressed by the apparent absence of elk, yet the first heavy autumnal snow will drive them from the mountains to the lowlands, the freshly fallen snow being tramped down by hundreds of elk tracks coming from all directions. In the more rugged portions of the country along the summit of the ridges, elk are seldom seen, although well-worn trails traverse the passes of the range at high altitudes, and may be safely followed by travelers as the easiest routes across the mountains.

A Mountain Pasture.
Photographed from life by W. H. Weed.

In an unexplored country, elk trails afford the best means of travel; they are well laid out and lead to good camping-grounds. Moreover, if there are any outlooks in the forest, or bare points on cliff or cañon wall, the trails will pretty surely take one there. I am much indebted to the elk for fine points of observation. Animals are not supposed to be lovers of nature. As regards the elk, this, I think, is an error. From long observation, I believe they have an appreciation of the picturesque and the grand. So thoroughly have I felt this that frequently when encamped in some beautiful and secluded nook, I have strolled away from the noise of the camp with a firm belief that at dusk these animals would visit the spot, attracted by its beauties, if by nothing else.

Possibly there are sportsmen who, having shot their elk, are not again attracted toward them, as toward other big game; they are easily killed, and the shooting of them becomes slaughter. Deer and antelope are more graceful and less easy to get a shot at than elk. Mountain sheep offer far more excitement in the chase over rugged cliffs. White goats are seldom seen, save in limited areas and out-of-the-way regions. Buffalo are now so rarely seen that to come upon one in the wilds is the ambition of the hunter. Bear-hunting must always be exciting on account of the element of danger. Preferring not to use the rifle, the pleasures of the chase do not enter into my enjoyment of animal life, and to me elk are the most interesting of all big game, and a constant source of pleasure. I never tire of watching them, they show so much individuality and independence of character and stateliness of manner. In spite of the fact that they are gregarious and fond of companionship, they show less affection for each other than almost any other animal.

I have much feeling in common with an old Scotch friend of mine, a lover of nature and a frequenter of forest and mountain, who spent a fortnight in the Park with the express purpose of reproducing upon his bagpipe those remarkable notes, the whistling of the elk, but with only partial success. The story is told that the elk left that part of the country, and he was unable to keep up with them.

That there are several thousand elk in the Park and adjoining country is quite certain, but from the nature of the case it is a difficult matter to estimate them. Their number may vary from year to year, depending upon the severity of the winter and other causes. Exceptionally severe seasons would naturally cause an increased death-rate. At all events, they exist in numbers sufficient to put at rest all fear of extermination if they shall only be protected and allowed to wander undisturbed. Several favorable seasons might cause them to reach the limit of a winter's food supply, but overcrowding must tend to a high death-rate, and the struggle for existence would keep their number down. The migratory habits of the elk would lead them to seek new haunts beyond the protected region, offering every year opportunities for healthy, manly sport to the ambitious hunter during the shooting-season.

Moose have been observed in this region only to a limited degree, but probably they occur in somewhat larger numbers than is generally supposed. While they are migratory in habit, their requirements restrict their favorite haunts to limited and inaccessible areas, and they prefer swampy and boggy regions in the lowlands to the meadows and grassy parks of the uplands. They roam mainly in the southwest corner of the Park, in the Falls River Basin, a level country fed by innumerable streams and springs coming out from beneath the lavas of the plateau. As this basin lies partly in Idaho, beyond the borders of the Park, and the moose wander in and out of the reservation, their protection is a matter of great difficulty; yet it is important, not only on account of their scarcity, but because it is near the southern limit of their range. They do not travel in large bands, and a country tramped up by moose is unknown in the Park. In many instances they have probably been mistaken for elk. I have detected their footprints in the broad valley of the Snake, below the mouth of Lewis River, and also in the Lower Geyser Basin, on Sentinel Creek, a small area, but one admirably fitted for their needs. They have been seen on the borders of the Lake of the Woods, and on the head of Stinking Water River east of Yellowstone Lake.

Two varieties of deer inhabit the Park, commonly known as the black-tail and white-tail deer, the former being much the more abundant of the two. Being fleet of foot, they roam over the entire area in passing from one pasturage ground to another. They show a decided preference for gently sloping foot-hills carrying a scattered growth of mingled pine and maple and other deciduous trees, their natural habitat being the border-land between dense forest and open valley. Such favorite spots affording food, shelter, and shade abound, and present one of the most characteristic features of an ideal park country. Deer haunt the valleys of the Gallatin Range and the lava slopes around the head of Black Tail Deer Creek, which flows into the Yellowstone; but more than any other animal they seem to delight in changing their habitat. The ideal country for deer is that paradise for big game, the valleys of the numerous streams forming the sources of the Snake. While by no means as numerous as elk, deer are found in sufficient numbers to allay all anxiety as to their permanence under the new conditions now surrounding the Park.

Antelope, graceful and swift-footed creatures, restrict their range to the open country, with habits nearly identical to those developed on the plain. They are by no means numerous, and were so much shot at before protection was afforded that they nearly became extinct. But in the last few years they have steadily increased in numbers, and experience seems to have taught them that safety lies within the protected region, rather than in seeking in winter the lowlands outside its borders. Swan Valley and the slopes of Mount Everts apparently satisfy their requirements. In summer small bands roam over Hayden Valley, but so far as I know have not increased in size.

The advantages of this region as a game reservation are again shown in its meeting the requirements of the bighorn, or mountain sheep (*Ovis canadensis*), an animal of quite different habits, which lives almost wholly among the crags and cliffs of the steepest mountains. An ideal bighorn country is found in the Absaroka Range, where the bare rocky slopes are interspersed with patches of nutritious grasses. The size of their bands, the frequent well-worn trails over the barren rocks, and the occurrence of sheep "sign" everywhere, indicate conditions suitable to sheep life. The head waters of the Stinking Water and Thoroughfare Creek are among their favorite haunts. In the higher regions of the Gallatin they may occasionally be seen, and, indeed, this may be said of the summits of most of the peaks throughout the Park. They are an agile, wary, keen-scented animal, and apparently never so happy as when on the jump. Next to the elk, they are probably most sought by the horn-hunters and game-butchers; but with a little protection, and only half a show, they are abundantly capable of taking care of themselves.

That buffalo were among the animals inhabiting the Yellowstone Park was known in the early days of its history; and that indefatigable explorer and former superintendent of the Park, Colonel P. W. Norris, soon recognized the need of protection for them if their extermination was to be prevented. The Park buffalo may all be classed under the head of mountain buffalo, and even in this elevated region they live for the greater part of the year in the timber. In many ways their habits are quite different from those generally attributed to the buffalo of the plain, and it is most unusual, save in midwinter, to find them in open valley or on the treeless mountain slope. They haunt the most inaccessible and out-of-the-way places, and what would seem to be the least attractive spots, living in open glades and pastures, the oases of the dense forest, often only to be reached by climbing over a tangle of fallen timber. Localities least visited by man and avoided by other animals are by preference selected by buffalo. During long wanderings over the timber plateau I have never ceased to be amazed at the resorts selected by them, and by the rapidity of their disappearance on being alarmed. I have frequently come upon ground tramped up by buffalo, showing every evidence of recent occupation, but the animals were gone. It is surprising how few buffalo have been seen in midsummer, even by those most familiar with their haunts and habits. They wander about in small bands in such unfrequented country as the southern end of the Madison plateau, the Mirror plateau, and the head of Pelican Creek, and on the borders of that elevated table-land known as Elephant Back. In winter, leaving the forest, they feed over the slopes of Specimen Ridge, and in the open Hayden Valley.

It is not likely that there ever were many buffalo in the Park, or that those there ever suffered seriously from the hand of man other than the Indian. Up to within recent years the plains buffalo offered a more attractive field for the hunter nearer home. Their abodes in the Park were inaccessible and far away from any base of supplies. Only since their extermination from the plains and the advance of settlements to the Park border have inroads upon their numbers taken place. If they ever roamed over this country in large herds, evidence of the fact should be apparent by well-trodden buffalo trails, which nowhere form a feature of the Park plateau. Whether the natural increase in their numbers has been kept down by the severity of the climate and an uncongenial environment, or whether the young calves have been attacked by predatory animals, has never been satisfactorily determined. Dangers which would scarcely befall them in an open country might in a timbered region tend to keep down their numbers. They occasionally wander beyond the Park borders into Idaho and Montana with the first fall of snow, returning to their mountain homes with the approach of spring. In 1884 I estimated the buffalo in the Park at 200; since that time they have gradually increased, and have probably doubled in number. In the winter of 1891-92 the grazing-ground in Hayden Valley was visited by a snowshoe party, who counted the scattered bands and took photographs of several groups. These groups were generally small, and each contained a goodly number of calves. They numbered by actual count nearly 300, but there is no means of knowing what proportion of the Park buffalo were then gathered here.

**Buffalo Cows and Calves.
Photographed from life by John Fossam. From Forest and Stream.**

Bears of all kinds that inhabit the northern Rocky Mountains are found in the Park. The natural conditions of the country—a dense pine forest; a soil producing a variety of wild fruits, berries, and roots; a slowly decaying vegetation upon which flourish grubs and ants, delicate morsels to Bruin—all tend to furnish an environment suitable to the omnivorous bear. Black bears are the most common, but silver-tips abound, many of them of great size and strength. They are undoubtedly increasing in numbers, but unless attacked are harmless; and of the thousands of visitors to the Park every year I have yet to learn of one injured by them.

Of the smaller animals, such as the different kinds of the *Felidæ*,— including mountain-lions,—foxes, wolves, porcupines, nothing need be said, save that they find within the reservation the essential conditions of a home. Two animals, however,—the wolverene and the beaver,— demand more than mere mention: the former on account of its rarity in the Rocky Mountains, and the consequent danger it runs of extermination, and the latter on account of the never-failing interest which they excite in the tourist, and the frequency with which their dams and habitations may be seen along the traveled routes. The wolverene is now seldom, if ever, reported from the country south of the Park, and must be considered one of the rarest of animals within its borders. Its predatory nature renders it a most undesirable animal near settlements, but this is no good reason why it should not be protected in the mountains. It is a stealthy, cautious animal, moving about without the least noise. I have seen but four, and these on meadow-lands underlaid by a deep soil. As they are supposed to live largely on rodents, they were doubtless seeking food among the burrowing animals. Although they are regarded as great robbers, in the hundreds of camps I have pitched within the Park my attention has never been called to the tracks of a prowling wolverene.

The numerous broad, flat valleys, cut into the plateaus and mountains, are singularly well fitted for the home of beaver. The meadows filling these valleys, the clear streams flowing through them, and the seclusion which they offer, are exceptional inducements and are all necessary requirements for their haunts. With the growth of population it is probable that a very considerable amount of trapping was carried on in early days, and their numbers greatly reduced. Of late years, special vigilance has been exercised to prevent the trapping and molestation of the Park beaver, but it has been by no means easy to accomplish this, on account of the remoteness of many of the best-stocked streams, and the high price of the skins, which tempts the cupidity of the trapper. Captain George S. Anderson, the present superintendent of the Park, believes the beaver are steadily increasing, and this is no doubt the fact, in view of the efforts that he has made to stop all trapping.

Innumerable streams flowing from the mountains to the central plateau, magnificent lakes, the sources of grand rivers, and a river system divided into four drainage basins, make the region singularly well suited for fish life. Exploration soon developed the fact that, while many of these rivers and lakes abounded in trout, others, above the waterfalls which form so characteristic a feature of the streams between the plateau and the lowlands, were wholly destitute of fish. In the spring of 1887 I addressed a letter to the late Professor Baird, calling his attention to the importance of stocking these waters, more especially Shoshone Lake, for the benefit of the people. At that time it was not considered feasible to take up the matter. Since then these waters have undergone careful investigation, and, as a result, have been stocked with fish under the supervision of Professor B. W. Evermann, of the United States Fish Commission, who reports that the different species of trout planted are doing well, so far as can be told at this early date. Six varieties—brook, lake, mountain, rainbow, Loch Leven, and Von Behr trout—have been placed in one or the other of the different drainage basins. In Shoshone and Lewis lakes both the common lake trout and the Loch Leven variety were planted. The Yellowstone Park is destined to rank as one of the favorite resorts of the angler,—fishing, under the proper regulations, becoming one of the many attractions of the place.

Nearly all birds common to the northern Rocky Mountains resort to this region during certain portions of every year. Migratory birds, like ducks and geese, live for months upon many small lakes dotted over the Park, rearing their young without the least fear of molestation. Pelicans find a home around the shores of Yellowstone Lake and the bottom-lands of its tributaries. That graceful creature and rare bird, the white swan, may frequently be seen on Yellowstone Lake, and on three separate visits to that secluded sheet of water, Riddle Lake, I have never failed to find several of them paddling about in its quiet waters. Eagles, fish-hawks, and ospreys soar above the forest, building their nests upon the summits of the crags and pinnacles in the wildest and most inaccessible places. It is always an impressive sight to see that magnificent bird, the bald-headed eagle, flying high over the lakes, crossing and recrossing the wooded continental watershed, equally at home among the sources of the Mississippi and Columbia, undisturbed by his only really dangerous enemy, rifle-bearing man.

The preservation of animal life, as it exists to-day under natural conditions within a government reservation, may be purely a matter of sentiment; but surely this grand possession must be worth every effort to preserve it, even at considerable cost of time and money. With the encroachments of civilization, the demands of those seeking to use the Park for their own selfish ends must in the nature of things steadily increase. Pressure for timber and water privileges, and rights of way for railroad purposes, will constantly arise. The larger part of the timber reservation should become an integral part of the Park, as much of the game, and its best breeding-grounds, lie within this reservation. Let Congress adjust the boundaries in the best interests of the Park and the needs of traffic, clearly defining them in accordance with the present knowledge of the country, and then forever keep this grand national reservation intact. After this is done, the Park can be maintained only by the constant vigilance of enthusiastic friends, who realize its value for economic reasons, and believe in the purposes of the organic act setting it apart forever as a pleasure-ground for the people.

Arnold Hague.

A Mountain Fraud

My acquaintance with Lanahan began at Eagle Rock, Idaho, in August, 1890, where we met to undertake a trip into Jackson's Hole. Mr. Melville Hanna and I had come from the east to make a hunt, and Lanahan had been engaged to purchase and superintend our outfit by a railway official at Boise, whom he had impressed with a belief in his remarkable fitness for both purposes.

When we reached Eagle Rock, Lanahan was on hand with eight packhorses, an elderly man called Mason, and an Englishman as cook. The cook claimed to have practised his vocation in the service of a duke on land, and an admiral on the deep, each of whom parted from him with a grief he was unable to conceal. He had come west for recreation and from a desire to see the country, was accustomed to riding, consequent upon having followed the hounds with his ducal employer, and intended, after seeing us safely back from our trip, to return to the assistance of the admiral, whose ship was on the way to Halifax. On inspecting Lanahan's list of supplies, we found that he had bought a good-sized stove and an assortment of delicacies such as I am sure never started for Jackson's Hole before. There were oysters put up in various ways, tins of cauliflower, peas, all the fruits of the Occident, and numerous exotic preserves which we had never heard of. The array looked too great for our eight horses to carry, and when we started next day this proved to be the fact.

Lanahan was a big burly fellow with a most repulsive countenance and with great powers of conversation. He had lived so long in the West that he had lost the manner of speech of his native isle, except when excited or frightened, and he regaled us the evening before starting with thrilling tales of his personal exploits with Indians and wild beasts. He professed to have passed years as the confidential scout of Howard, Custer, and Crook, and the last named owed the fame he had attained as an Indian-fighter to his implicit adherence to Lanahan's advice on several critical occasions. As to game, he had fairly wallowed in the gore of bears and lions, and he promised to escort me to my first encounter with a silver-tip, the death of which was to be brought about by my opening fire on him at 600 yards and keeping it up during the ensuing charge, Lanahan standing by peacefully until the bear rose to embrace me, when he would give him the *coup de grâce* with "Old Nance," as he fondly called his rifle. He also announced his intention of shooting any Indians who might come to our camp, if they did not promptly leave at his bidding.

Next morning Mason and Lanahan began packing, and Lanahan showed by the humility with which he endured the deserved abuse of Mason that he was as ignorant of the art as we afterward found him of every other, except that of dissimulation. Mason was finally obliged to substitute our cook as helper, and Lanahan, in order to recover his prestige, spoke of the dangerous character of the horse-thieves of Jackson's Hole, and showed a map of the country made by old Jackson himself, then languishing in Boise jail, also a letter from the same hand introducing Lanahan to the present head of the association, who would, on its presentation, protect our stock and return without cost any that had previously been stolen. At starting, Hanna and I went on ahead, and were presently joined by Mason and the cook with the packs; but as Lanahan did not appear, we sent back Mason, who produced him in about an hour, quite flushed as to his countenance and uncertain as to his speech, but with that part of his intellect devoted to lying as unclouded as ever. His delay, he stated, had been caused by his horse rearing and falling on him, whereat he became so faint from pain that he was unable to move until after a long rest and the administration of a teaspoonful of the best brandy every fifteen minutes. About this time the packs began to loosen and get lopsided, and one of the pack-horses, called Emigrant, would occasionally lie down, and have to be assisted to his feet by the united strength of the party. We were able to keep him going only by having the cook lead him while Hanna and I beset him with blows in the rear.

In consequence of these misfortunes, our progress was so slow that we made camp that night only six miles from our starting-point. The next night we reached Big Butte Ferry, the trouble about the packs keeping up, and Emigrant growing more and more averse to the exertions required from him. At this point we "cached" the stove, stovepipe, and half a dozen of our most useless pots and pans despite the remonstrances of our cook, and engaged a young man named Joe, who had been out for a month prospecting for coal, but was quite willing to turn back with us. Reaching the village of Kaintuck at noon, we camped in the corral of the livery-stable, and in less than half an hour our cook betook himself to one of the neighboring saloons, where we shortly found him so drunk as to be incapable of speech or motion, but—as we judged from never seeing him again—still able to understand that he was discharged.

During the afternoon we fell into conversation with a bright, active-looking fellow who came to call on us; and, finding that he was familiar with the Teton country, had hunted and trapped around Jackson's Lake, and claimed to be an expert packer and first-class cook, we added him to our party in these capacities. Later, Lanahan came to us in great agitation, and said that Harrington, our new man, was a very dangerous character, and had just been pardoned from jail, where he was serving a twenty-five years' sentence for horse-stealing; that he had broken out once, and had been recaptured only after an exciting chase of seventy-five miles, during which he had been shot in the leg. We asked Harrington about this. He admitted its substantial truth, but said he was innocent of the crime, and had been the victim of malicious persecution by some men who wanted to "jump" his ranch in the Teton valley; so we decided to take him along, and did not regret it. The disposition by sale for $20 of a large quantity of our delicacies to the Mormon storekeeper at Kaintuck lessened the weight of our packs, which Harrington made up next morning in less than half the usual time, to the evident disgust of Lanahan and Mason. Before leaving the town, Harrington took me to a saloon where hung several drawings he had made of elk and Indians, which were as true to nature in their general features as anything of the kind I have ever seen, and caused me to believe that he only needed education to make him distinguished. He had never had any instruction, and his only artistic implement was a lead-pencil.

When we reached the Teton Valley, Lanahan, who had taken up riding ahead to "look out the trail," which was as definite as Broadway, and to protect us against the dangers which encompassed our path, learned from a passer-by that fifty lodges of Lemhi Indians were before us on a hunt. He called Hanna and me to one side, when he conveyed this information, and said he was now convinced of what he had suspected from the first, that Harrington's joining us was part of a plot between him and the Lemhis to facilitate the running off of our horses, and an incidental murder or two, if necessary. That night we camped on the west side of Mount Hayden, the biggest of the Tetons, close by the place where the Indians had stayed a few days before; and Lanahan armed himself and climbed a little peak at some distance from the trail to "look for Indian signs," as he said. At the fire, after supper, he informed us that years ago he was well acquainted with old Teton, after whom the mountains were named, and who had lived in the valley when it was fairly alive with game.

The Grand Teton, now so wretchedly mis-named, is to my mind the most magnificent of mountains. Its situation, its isolation from neighbors, its great height, its vast hollows and chasms, many of them filled with perpetual snow, and its lofty, bare, inaccessible peak, always impress me with a sense of grandeur, majesty, and beauty, such as I have never found in any other mountain.

About this time Lanahan abandoned all activity except looking for Indians, poisoning our minds against Harrington, and attempting the "horse-wrangling" each morning. He would start out alone quite early, and after blundering about in a most inefficient way, and getting all the nervous horses thoroughly excited and scared, would call some of the other men to his assistance, and then proceed himself to get the packs in as great confusion as possible before the horses were brought in, the one or two that he had caught meantime having escaped.

The next night, before we crossed the divide into Jackson's Hole through Trail Creek Cañon, we had a very heavy thunder-storm, and in the intervals between the peals we could hear Lanahan's vociferous invocations to the various saints he relied upon for protection, his appeals mingling with the damning he was getting from his tent-mates for the disturbance he created. He was so much demoralized by the storm, and by the chance of overtaking the Indians, who were evidently not far ahead of us, that he endured all this abuse with perfect meekness, and did not recover his usual intrepid bearing until the next noon, when he resumed his ostentatious superintendence of the outfit.

Our first camp after crossing the divide was at Fighting Bear Creek, and was made memorable by killing a two-year-old bull elk, the toughest of his race; but fresh meat had become so desirable that his india-rubber qualities were not unfavorably criticized until we got something better.

A man coming down the valley told us that the band of Indians had divided, most of them going south, and ten or twelve men and squaws northward, in the direction we were to take. This somewhat reassured

Lanahan, though he strongly advised staying where we were for a time, and then striking east into the Gros Ventre Mountains, where he knew of great quantities of game. The stranger also told us of the disappearance of Mr. Robert Ray Hamilton from his new ranch at the upper crossing of Snake River.

We made our permanent camp directly under the peak of the Grand Teton, on the east side. It was in a little park surrounded by pines. Cottonwood Creek, a beautiful sparkling stream, flowed through it, and above us were the grand mountain masses, feeding from their snow-clad sides the chain of little lakes along their bases, which in turn replenish the mighty Snake River during all the rainless summer months. I have never seen so delightful a camping-ground, nor one which supplied so completely every requisite for comfort and sport. Our hunting adventures during the next ten days in this camp were not remarkable, though we might have killed a large amount of game had we desired. There were a great many antelope out on the prairie, and every morning we could see some in the park. I once aroused the curiosity of a solitary buck to the point of coming up within thirty yards of me by concealing myself in the sage-brush and waving about my wide-brimmed hat on the end of my rifle. We found antelope liver the choicest delicacy to be had in the Rockies, and this fact perhaps led us to kill one or two more of these graceful and interesting creatures than we should otherwise have done.

It was hardly late enough for the bull elk to come down from the high ranges to join the cows and calves. Two large bands of these ranged between us and Jackson's Lake, about fourteen miles north. We could have shot some of these almost daily, but one of the men, contrary to our orders, having gone out and killed two calves soon after our arrival, Hanna and I agreed, after he had shot one cow, not to fire at anything except bulls, and we were guiltless of the blood of any more elk during our stay. One day, near Jackson's Lake, Harrington and I came to a salt-lick in the woods, which we approached quietly, thinking game might be there. When we reached the edge, we saw a big cow elk standing among the trees on the other side of the open space, and directly after, another one lying down in the high grass near the first, only her head and neck being visible. She saw us, but did not stir. Keeping perfectly still and looking closely, we discovered seven or eight more, but none with horns. Finally, stepping forward, thinking we had seen them all, a great number jumped up, going out like a covey of quail. Some had been lying down in the high grass within twenty yards of us, and could not have known of our presence. They made a great noise and crashing as they scurried off, and we could only guess at their numbers, but there must have been thirty or forty.

There were not many bears about here. We saw the tracks of several very big ones, but only four living ones. One of these disappeared before we could get a shot, and the other three, an old cinnamon with two well-grown cubs, we found at the top of one of the lower peaks of the Grand Teton near camp. It had taken Hanna and me three hours' hard climbing to get near the summit, where we expected to find some of the bull elk we had heard whistling, and the tracks of which we saw fresh and plentiful as we ascended.

We were moving very quietly along the game trail, Hanna ahead, when he suddenly stopped and pointed about seventy-five yards in front, where we saw the two cubs playing on some rocks overhanging a deep gulch. We fired nearly simultaneously. My cub dropped dead, while Hanna's, badly wounded, started up the mountain howling his best. It was not ten seconds before the mother appeared, not fifteen yards ahead of us, charging down the trail looking as big as a horse and growling savagely. Hanna, being a step in front of me, fired, and the bear dropped, but was up in an instant and came straight on. He shot again, and again she dropped, but was up like a rubber ball. The third time the cartridge failed to explode. The bear turned a little out of the trail, evidently bewildered, but as vicious as ever. As she passed me, within ten feet, I shot, and the ball pierced the heart, but it required two more of the 45-90 bullets to kill her. She was one of the long-legged greyhound kind, but quite fat; and, judging from the impression she made on a small tree she ran against and clawed like an angry cat, she would have badly damaged any man she might have met. Her jaw had been shattered by Hanna's first shot; the second had traversed her body, and there were two through her heart. Her vitality was really astonishing. We got the wounded cub, but the other had rolled down the gulch; and as we could not reach him without a long detour, we left him behind. We skinned the two animals and packed their hides to camp on our backs, finding the loads very heavy before we reached there.

Porcupines were very plentiful, as they are in most parts of the Rockies, and grow to a great size. They sometimes fall victims to bears, which manage to turn them over and get at the unprotected parts, eating everything but the quill-covered skin. In one day's hunt I saw the remains of three that had been thus treated. Bears also dig up the nests of yellow-jackets for the larvæ they contain; and we came upon a nest so lately rifled that many of its former occupants were still buzzing angrily about.

After pleasant days spent at this camp, we packed up and started north to go through the Yellowstone Park. As we were passing out of Jackson's Hole, we looked back and had a superb view of the great valley with the Snake River winding through it, the bare ranges of the Gros Ventre Mountains, and the towering snow-capped rocky peaks of the Tetons—a wonderful picture.

The day after leaving Marymere ranch, we saw, as we were making camp, three Indians watching us from a distant hill. Lanahan's consternation was extreme, and he declared that we must take turns watching through the night. As nobody paid much attention to him, except to encourage his going personally, he loaded his rifle, put on his cartridge-belt full of ammunition, and started out after supper ostensibly to guard us, but we felt sure to conceal himself somewhere in safety from the impending attack, which would have been welcome if it had bereaved us of him. Next morning he intimated that the savages had been prowling about, and that we owed the protection of our scalps to his vigilance. This idea of his was strengthened by the appearance, while we were breakfasting, of a Lemhi Indian on a beautiful pony. He could not or would not speak any English, and Harrington conversed with him in the sign-language, to our great interest, as we had never seen it used before.

Our journey to the Lower Geyser basin was unmarked by anything startling, though Lanahan was much discomposed one night by two men who had come down from the Stinking Water and camped near us. He was so convinced that they were in league with Harrington that he "watched" the horses all night. At the basin we started the outfit back to Boise with Lanahan and Mason, and joined our families, who were awaiting us. We heard afterward that Lanahan was a prey to the liveliest terrors while in the Park, and paid a man $10 to watch the horses the two nights before he got out of Harrington's reach. We have never heard of Lanahan since, but his memory will ever be green.

Dean Sage.

Blacktails in the Bad Lands

One bright, cold November day I started from a ranch on the Little Missouri, in western Dakota, with the set purpose of getting venison for the ever hungry cow-boys. They depended solely upon me for their supply of fresh meat; and as for some time I had shot nothing, I had been the subject of disparaging comment for several days, and the foreman, in particular, suggested that I should stay at home and kill a steer, and not chase all the black-tails into the next county.

So I stole off this time with an almost guilty conscience, and plunged at once into the dense brush of the river-bottom. In the thicket I startled a Virginia deer, but knew it to be one only by the waving salute of its white flag. I also passed a tree in one of the forks of which I had, at another time, found an old muzzle-loading rifle, rusted, worn, and decaying, a whole history in itself, and beyond, not two hundred yards away, an Indian's skull with a neat round hole through the crown.

The Keogh stage road crossed the river near by, and I found out that the place was the scene of the last Indian deviltry in this section. It was the old story. A man, while looking for the stage-horses, was shot; a second, hearing the report, went out to see what it meant, and was in turn killed; while a third, with perhaps a little more experience, jumped on the only horse left at the station and fled for his life, with half a dozen Indians in full cry in pursuit.

I walked on along the old trail taken by the lucky fugitive, and up out of the river-valley to a level plateau above. From the top could be seen in the distance several big buttes, and a dark pine-tree, which was to be my objective point for the day's hunt. To the right, as I stepped briskly forward, was a large washout, cut deep into the clay soil, broken and irregular, with sage-brush scattered here and there along its sides and bottom. At the head of the washout I spied some yellow long-horned Texas cattle, and gave them a wide berth. I had had some pleasing experiences of their habits, and did not care just then to be stamped flat.

To the left, a few hundred yards away, was a long valley leading to the river and far out into the prairie, wooded in patches, with small pockets at intervals along the sides, filled with low brush. Here at other times I had jumped whitetails from their daytime naps, and once had had a running shot at a large prairie-wolf. Bearing all this in mind, I veered over toward the valley, and had not gone far when I saw in the distance a black-tail buck come skipping out of it, and moving with high, long bounds, as is the way of its kind when frightened or going at speed.

These bounds, by the way, are very curious: the animal lands on all four feet at once, in such a small area that a sombrero would cover the four footprints. On a few occasions, when very badly frightened, I have seen them run level, like a race-horse; but that gait is so unusual as hardly to be considered characteristic of this deer. The deer in question, after a few long jumps, settled down into a trot, then into a walk, and finally stopped and looked about. He did not see me, however, and when he again moved off there was a man jogging quietly along in his wake.

Taking advantage of every little hollow to keep from his sight and make a spurt, I soon reduced the distance between us, and arrived at the further edge of the plateau just in time to see him disappear in some broken country. Continuing cautiously on to where I had last seen him, it became apparent that he had determined upon some definite course, for his tracks led as straight as the nature of the ground would permit to what I knew was the head of a large coulée which ran into the valley from which he had come into view.

As the soil was very hard and dry, and his tracks difficult to follow, I soon determined to leave them and cut straight for the coulée below the point toward which he had been headed, thinking it likely that he would continue his course down the coulée, at least for a short distance. I ought to be able to write that "events turned out exactly as calculated," but they did not. I ran with a fair burst of speed to the edge of the coulée, and when, after quietly watching for twenty minutes, no deer appeared, my mind went back to the foreman's remark about killing a steer.

However, it remained for me to go up to the point where it was probable the buck entered the coulée. I accordingly did so, hunting every inch of the way, and looking for sign and whatever else might turn up. I saw nothing, however, but two grouse that startled me, as they always do, but especially when my nerves are strung up as they were just then. What course the buck had taken, was now the question. Doubling back to my old conclusion that he had gone straight, I went out of the coulée, and followed on the line he had gone. At first it led over another small plateau, then it dipped down again into some more bad lands, cut up and broken with picturesque red scoria hills covered with straggling twisted cedar-trees.

About this time my ardor for this particular buck had begun to subside, and he was now anybody's game. Being somewhat tired as well, I climbed to the top of a round clay butte, sat down, and lighted a pipe. I had been smoking for about ten minutes, enjoying the mysterious scenery and thinking what course it would be best to take, when again my buck loomed up for a few seconds in the distance, and once more walked quickly out of sight. This was a great surprise and pleasure, and the pace at which I set out in pursuit would have rejoiced the heart of a messenger boy. I ran as fast as I could, stopping to peer over every rise in the land, and was soon rewarded by a most interesting sight. The buck had come upon another, fully as large if not larger than himself, and they were exchanging greetings across a small washout, each extending his nose and smelling the other. They would sniff a minute and then turn their heads about, flap their long gray ears, and wiggle their short black tails, acting as if they were old friends.

It seems a great pity to shoot such noble creatures; but unfortunately this thought rarely comes at the right time for the deer. Given, a man having killed nothing for several days, unmercifully guyed by all the cow-boys, and add to that a long and lively chase after constantly vanishing venison,—when, then, the man gets within shooting distance, it is hardly at such a time that his kindly instincts will suggest the propriety of letting the poor beasts escape.

As for myself, with every muscle and nerve at tension from an exciting chase, and mind fairly satisfied of game well earned, it would have taken more self-denial than I pretend to possess not to shoot, especially since we had been living on pork for some time. When fresh meat is plentiful in camp, it is to a real sportsman no sacrifice to let the does and fawns escape, or to shoot them merely with the deadly kodak; but on this day the shack really had to have meat—those lordly heads, too.

There is always a strong desire, when one comes upon game, to shoot at once; but it is a good plan, if possible, to rest and get one's breathing apparatus into proper shape. It is most exasperating, not to say cruel, to wound a deer and have him get away; and there is a good chance of this happening if, before your hand steadies and your head clears, you begin to open fire.

From the direction of the wind it was quite evident that the deer could not scent me, so for some moments I lay watching the animals with lively interest, and wondering what they would do next.

They were apparently satisfied with an occasional sniff at one another, but seemed at the same time to give their attention to something beyond my view. From my position on top of a small mound, or butte, where I had crawled with great caution, nothing could be seen either up or down a large washout that was between me and the deer; and I had poked my gun through a bunch of grass, and was quite prepared to shoot, when the ears, then the head and body, of a large doe, closely followed by a young buck and a yearling, came into full view.

To say that I was surprised but faintly expresses it, and for the time being all idea of shooting left me, as I watched with keenest interest the advent of the new-comers. The old doe, as if aware of her importance as the respected matron of a family, walked sedately past the two bucks without bestowing the least attention upon them, selected a grassy spot in the sun, pivoted around twice to level her bed, and quietly settled to earth, facing me. The young buck and yearling stood as if not quite decided whether to follow her example, but finally began to nibble grass and walk about. Here, indeed, was a pretty picture,—an embarrassment of riches. I thought it quite possible to get one big buck, with the chance of a good running shot at the other; and as there was no hurry, and my gun was at a dead rest for the first shot at least, I decided to shoot at the largest buck behind the ear, and then trust to occasion for whatever should follow.

Resting.
Photographed from life by T. G. Ingersoll. From Forest and Stream.

I felt that excitement was again about to get the upper hand, and I aimed carefully several times before pulling trigger. At last, after a sharp report, the smoke blew directly in my face, and for a second I could see nothing distinctly; but when it cleared away, and I, having pumped a cartridge into place, was again prepared to shoot, what was my astonishment to find that the buck fired at had utterly disappeared, and that the second, far from being frightened, was still standing with his nose poked down into the washout that had been between them.

Without further speculation, I sighted for the neck of buck number two, and at the report he also disappeared; but this time I made out that he fell over forward into the washout. Everything was now afoot and moving about, so taking a quick shot at the doe, behind the shoulder, and three more at the remaining two, the last on the jump, I realized, by seeing them fall, a big day's work, and for the moment felt very proud. It was not until afterward that the feeling came up that my glory would have been quite enough without killing the last three; but then it must be remembered that we needed every pound of meat at the shack.

The two big bucks had fallen into the washout, which was about six feet deep, one directly on top of the other, and it was beyond my strength, without a horse and rope, to pull them out. As it was, I had to clean them in very uncomfortable quarters and not in the most approved manner. During November, in the northern latitudes, the sun is early to bed, and it was four o'clock and getting gray when the last deer had been cared for. At dark I washed all trace of blood from my hands and arms in the river near the shack, and strolled into the kitchen with as woebegone a countenance as I could muster. I intended to get even with the foreman.

A sardonic smile stole over his face, and a disgusted look over those of the others, as they noticed my unstained hands. I remarked to the foreman that I had shot some game. He promptly replied, "You didn't; if you had, you'd have been so proud you'd be as red as a scoria butte with deer blood, to show off. No such luck; and as long as you and that thirty-eight-caliber pop-gun go rustling around this country, I reckon we'll eat pork and be — glad to get it."

To this I answered that if he would promise to pack in what game I had killed, and would do it, I would give him the hunting-knife that he had been trying to steal for the last week. He instantly called it a bargain, and asked how far it was to the game. I answered that it was about five miles, and that I would take him there in the morning.

So next morning we started on horseback, and I went far enough with him to point out exactly where the deer were, and leaving him, I rode over to call on a friend who had a small horse-ranch in the neighborhood. I stayed at this horse-ranch overnight, and did not get back to our ranch until the following evening about supper-time.

It leaked out that the cow-boys had fairly screamed with delight when the truth was known, and would rather have been discharged than help the foreman pack in the five deer. He did pack them, however, in good faith; and both he and the cow-punchers, now that they had fresh meat, spared me their jokes, and for several days did not try to lend me their pitching ponies.

Thus ended a most eventful hunt; and although it was unquestionably a very exceptional piece of good luck to have killed five deer neatly, still it is none the less a fact that with a thirty-eight-caliber rifle I have always done the best work. With a fifty-caliber I have shot deer in their vital parts and then had them run great distances, whereas with the smaller bullet, when properly hit, they would almost invariably double up on the spot. I can give no explanation that will help to determine why the smaller-bored rifle has always, with me, been the most efficient.

Bronson Rumsey.

Photographing Wild Game

The sportsman who wishes to substitute the camera for the rifle should possess not only a special knowledge of photography, but also many qualifications not absolutely necessary to a successful hunter. Any one who has had much experience in hunting large game will remember occasions when, if he had only had a camera, it would have been easy enough to have made successful pictures. But, once provided with a camera, and having started out with the sole object in view of making negatives, he will find the opportunities for successful work few and far between.

The true sportsman is not a game-butcher. When he has shot what he wants, he may well refuse to avail himself of chances to kill, and turn to the camera as a weapon with which to bring home trophies of his abilities as a hunter. Few indeed are the localities where hunters complain of being able to kill more game than they need; yet it has been my good fortune for a number of years to spend my annual vacation in a country where game is so abundant that little effort is needed to provide camp with the needed fresh meat.

Having in years gone by, through force of circumstances, acquired a thorough technical knowledge of photography, it naturally occurred to me to attempt the use of the camera when there was no need for a rifle. Although I had such a knowledge of photography and of the habits of the game as had always enabled me to meet with fair success in the use of either camera or rifle, I had no adequate idea of the difficulties of my undertaking until they became real from actual experience. My first effort was with a small and excellent hand camera, which also served to make views of camp scenes and the beautiful scenery of the country in which I was hunting. I was especially fortunate in that my hunting-ground was on some one of the great park plateaus of northwestern Colorado.

These plateaus are indeed the sportsman's paradise. They comprise numerous great parks, forests of timber, and lakes ranging in size from the tiny pool of brown snow-water to those large enough to deserve a name and a place on the map. They are the great summer home of the deer and elk. Frequent rains cause a most abundant growth of herbage suitable for their food, and the higher ground provides cool retreats for the male deer and elk while their horns are growing and hardening. They never leave these plateaus until driven down by the snow. Here elk and deer have for the past few years existed in sufficient numbers to give abundant sport. Farther to the north, where these plateaus break into the sage-brush plains of Wyoming, antelope inhabit the larger parks, and from these feed up for some distance through more open timber on the slopes of the surrounding hills. In this more northerly locality I have succeeded in getting photographs of elk, antelope, and deer, all within a distance of but a few miles.

My first experience with an ordinary camera soon showed me that, at the usual distances, pictures of game would be so small as to be of no use. With a year's experience to guide me, I began the construction of a camera especially adapted for the purpose in view. For my lens I used a Dallmeyer rapid rectilinear, whole-plate size. I used only the back combination of the lens, which gave a focal length of about twenty-two inches. The lens was equipped with a Prosch duplex shutter, which was, I found, even when set for its lowest speed, too rapid for my purpose. In determining upon a camera, I had already arrived at the following conclusions: the camera must be a hand camera, equipped with a film-roll holder; it must be water-proof, light, not easily damaged, and of small size—*i.e.*, must make only a small-sized negative; focusing must be done at the front by moving the lens.

To obtain these conditions, I constructed my first camera in the following manner: I made a rectangular core of wood exactly the shape I wished the inside of my camera to be. The front end of this core was cylindrical. I then built up on this core of wood a paper shell, using strong Manila paper saturated with shellac as it was rolled upon the core. This was then wound with a strong cord at intervals of about one half inch, in order to provide cell spaces and consequently stiffness; and over all was stretched strong muslin, fastened to the core with liquid glue. The outside was then shellacked until it was absolutely smooth and hard, when the wooden core was removed, and there remained a paper tube which admirably met my requirements. A wooden frame, fitted to the larger end, received the roll holder, and the cylindrical part of the front received a brass tube covered with velvet, to the end of which was soldered the lens flange. This tube could be easily moved in and out of the end, while the friction of the velvet always kept it in place. Upon this tube I marked the focus for various distances. Of course the lens was capable of making a much larger picture than my roll holder would receive, and the surplus light was cut off by a metal diaphragm placed inside of the tube.

I found that this camera, when provided with a strap, could be carried slung on the shoulder with very little trouble.

The slowness of the lens I found a drawback, and after a year's experience I obtained a 12-15 Dallmeyer single-combination lens, which I had mounted in aluminum, thereby saving considerable weight. For this lens I constructed a camera on a different principle, as the length was too great to carry conveniently in the form of a rigid apparatus. This in turn I have displaced with a Dallmeyer telephoto lens, mounted in aluminum, which I consider a marvelous instrument.

I have not succeeded in obtaining any pictures with it as yet. The difficulties of using it are in some respects greater than with the other lenses, as it requires to be focused on the object. I have, however, designed a camera with the ground glass fastened rigidly in the top, and with a movable mirror which permits of the focus being obtained without removing the roll holder. This camera, when extended, is thirty inches long, and when packed for carrying is reduced one half.

It is home-made; but, if constructed by experienced workmen, I believe would very satisfactorily fill the conditions necessary for a game-camera. The weight and size, together with the necessity of focusing, require, however, some kind of a support. I believe that a pair of adjustable legs, with a universal joint which could be easily attached to the front of the camera, and a small handle by which the back could be supported by the hand and moved in any required direction, would answer every purpose. The image made by this lens is so large, and the field comparatively so small, that it requires the facility and precision of sighting which are obtained in the rifle. I use no finders, preferring sights exclusively.

With this incomplete sketch of a hunting photographer's weapons, let us consider the conditions under which he must capture his game; and suppose him in pursuit of the king of all stags, the noble elk,—giving him the advantage even of being in hearing of the clear bugle-note which never fails to thrill the hunter who has once heard it and so knows its significance. To make a successful stalk with a rifle, he would simply get his game between himself and the wind, and approach with such caution, and under such cover, as circumstances permitted. When once within gunshot, ninety-nine times out of one hundred he might make a successful termination to the stalk, without ever seeing more of his game, before firing, than a patch of brown as large as his hat. The swaying of the white antler-tips in the midst of the thicket, the particular shade of the moving brown seen through the openings, would almost always disclose the location of the vital point to the eye of the experienced, where the tyro would distinguish nothing but the shadow of the thicket, moving twigs, and the browns and russets of bark and leaves.

Under such circumstances as these, while the hunter triumphantly raises his rifle, the photographer crouches hopeless and discouraged. Far different conditions are needed for a successful result of his undertaking. Not only must the wind be in his face, but the sun must be at his back, or upon either side. He must be in dense cover, and yet cover that permits the free range of his lens. His game must be in the open, without intervening objects, and must be in the broad glare of sunshine. The hunter never realizes how seldom an animal comes into full view until he has followed him around with a camera, and met with failure after failure, after having had numbers of chances which with a rifle would have put a speedy end to the chase. When the bull elk are whistling they are an easy animal to stalk; yet I should consider it an easier task by far to kill fifty full-grown bulls than to obtain a picture of one which would combine photographic perfection with satisfactory composition.

He who follows game with a camera, and who feels the satisfaction of matching his faculties against those of his game, will, however, derive a keen sporting enjoyment from his failures; and if he meets with success, great will be his pride and contentment. He will learn much about the habits of game which has escaped him before; and, not needing to use his rifle, his opportunities for observation will be more frequent and satisfactory. For myself, the few pictures that comprise the results of my hunting with the camera have brought me a keener enjoyment and a greater sense of satisfaction than the finest heads in my collection, possibly on the ground that we are disposed to value most that which has cost us most.

I succeeded in obtaining a satisfactory photograph of some antelope one morning, when we were on the homeward journey from one of my hunts. I had ridden on ahead of the pack-train, and was just coming to the edge of the timber when I saw the white spots of several antelope feeding in the sage-brush just beyond. Tumbling off my horse, I crept along until as near as I deemed safe, when I stood up behind the trunk of a tree and, pointing my camera through an opening, made a noise to attract the attention of the antelope. They lifted their heads, and with a quick snap I had captured them. They remained motionless, and turning my roll to get another film, I found I had used the last one. With careful and slow development, I obtained a fair negative. I had judged the distance to be seventy-five yards, and the focus showed that I was nearly correct.

My most successful attempt at elk was made the year following, when, after two weeks of stormy, bad weather, during which I had seen abundance of game, but had had no chance to photograph, I started off, with a pack-animal and one man, to make a quiet camp ten miles away, where I knew there were plenty of elk. When we had gone as far as we dared, we pitched camp in a little park, and picketing our pack-animals, started to reconnoiter. I found an abundance of fresh tracks and wallows, and finally saw two young bull elk feeding in the open. The only point which would enable me to get near them with a fair light, required me to get very nearly in line with the wind; but as there was nothing else to be done, I determined to chance it. When I arrived at this point, I found that in feeding they had walked farther away, and I was obliged to crawl over the intervening space. We had nearly accomplished this when the circling of the wind gave them an inkling of our presence, and put them on the alert. We remained quiet, hoping that the wind would change back; but it did not, and they stole away into the thicket.

About three o'clock we caught sight of a twelve-point bull coming out to drink. I could have snapped at him with a downward shot, as I was on the slope above him; but as the distance was great, I decided to try and get nearer. He walked in behind some willows and, as I discovered afterward, lay down in some water to take his mud-bath. While this was going on I began to slide down the hill, watching for his reappearance, when to my surprise and disgust I suddenly saw the head and horns of an elk that was lying down one hundred yards to my right and almost on a level with me. I did not want to disturb him, with a chance of startling all the other elk in the neighborhood before I had a chance to photograph them, and so decided to try and get a photograph of his head and horns. With my man George following at my heels, I finally crept up behind a low spruce-tree about seventy-five feet from his highness. I knew from experience, however, that his head and horns would be almost undistinguishable on the negative against the surrounding objects. Getting my camera ready, and leaning out from behind the bush, I told George to whistle so that the elk would get up. To my great surprise, he turned his head in our direction and, without rising, gave vent to a shrill blast of defiance or annoyance, as it seemed. After repeating these tactics several times, and finally shouting at him, only to meet with the same answer, I finally decided to stand up, in the hope that when he arose he would hesitate an instant and give me an opportunity. Upon performing my part of the program, he gave one look in my direction, sprang to his feet, and was off with such rapidity that, although I snapped the shutter, the resulting negative showed only an undistinguishable blur, due partly to his motion and partly to my haste in trying to make a quick exposure.

We then followed in the direction of the large band, the bulls of which were making a great deal of noise. I finally located them about half a mile away in the heavy timber. The shadows then were very long in the open space, and I knew there was no use of trying to photograph except in the open. As a forlorn hope I told George to hurry through the timber and get on the other side of the band, while I would stand in the open space, so that I might get a snap shot if they came through. In a short time I heard a commotion in the band, and a sharp stampede in different directions, accompanied by loud bugling by the head of the band, whose voice was so deep and sonorous that I readily recognized it as the one I had heard a few nights previous in the same locality. At that time my companion and I had christened him the "elk with the foghorn." In the midst of the commotion, George gave vent to several startling yells, which I supposed were made in his effort to turn the band.

In a short time he returned, breathless and tired. As soon as he was able to speak, he recounted a tale of wonder which can readily be imagined by any of the readers of this chapter for whom George has acted in the multiple capacity of guide, cook, philosopher, and friend. He said that when the band got his wind, after several short stampedes, they dashed directly toward him, and as I had made him leave his rifle with me, he had no alternative except to climb a tree or jump out where he could be seen and swing his arms and yell. He said that this stopped the band, but the old bull with the fog-horn walked directly toward him until he thought he was going to charge, and looked for a convenient tree. After inspecting George, however, the bull walked off with his band, apparently not much alarmed. George and I returned to camp with nothing to show for a hard day's work, cooked our supper, and tumbled into our blankets.

A starlight night gave promise of a perfect day on the morrow, and we arranged to get up before daylight, so as to catch the elk before they had lain down. The next day the same experience was repeated: not a photographic shot came in our way, and about three o'clock we went back to camp weary and disgusted. As we had to be in the main camp that night, ready to start back home the next day, we loaded our pack-mule and were soon on the back trail. About half-past four we suddenly heard an elk whistle, not far to the left. We were going on a game-trail, through heavy timber, and I remarked to George, "This is our last chance." We quickly tied our animals and rushed in the direction of the call.

A few hundred yards brought us out on a little projection, and, cautiously looking over, we saw that the ground sloped up beyond through burned timber, and that there was a band of elk scattered around feeding. Adjusting my lens to the distance, which I judged to be one hundred yards, I made one exposure after another as rapidly as possible. The bull was not in sight, but we could hear him crashing around through the thicker timber, and bellowing in anger at another elk in the distance.

Suddenly, to my great delight, I saw his majesty come into the opening and walk rapidly across between the trees. There was only one opening large enough to show his whole body, and into this I pointed my camera; but as one of the cows had already got sight of us, I knew that my opportunities were short. As the bull entered the opening, I was as near an attack of buck-fever as ever before. The resulting picture shows a slight movement of the camera; but although the sun was very low, I succeeded with careful development in getting this and several other satisfactory negatives. I also had my small camera with me, and made several exposures; but the elk can be distinguished only by spots like the head of a pin, if at all. In the mean time one of the cows had fed up very close to us, and suddenly stopped in the shadow and looked at us. I made an exposure on her, but the negative showed nothing. A second more, and with a spring she was off, and suddenly the whole band dashed away in a tumult of crashing sticks and timber. Hurrying on in the direction of the other elk, I started to cross a stream under some dense alders, when suddenly a yearling cow started away and, running around, stopped directly in front of the opening, in an attitude of listening and looking back. I quickly reduced my lens to a shorter focus and made an exposure which gave a fair picture, although the position was an unusual one. This ended my opportunities for the day and trip.

These negatives show a remarkable blending in the color of the elk and their surroundings, and they would be quite difficult to distinguish were it not that some were in sunlight, with a shadowy background. One negative shows nine cows, nearly all feeding.

In photographing elk, I very soon learned that they do not like to come out into the openings during the middle of the day; consequently, when one gets opportunities, the light is so non-actinic that the results are apt to be very much undertimed. Ordinarily, a rapid shot is not needed for photographing game, as when there is any opportunity at all, they are either moving slowly or standing still. I should say just enough speed is required to neutralize any unavoidable motion of the camera which might take place during the exposure.

While trying to photograph the does and fawns which were continually jumping up and running away as we rode along from day to day, I observed a very curious habit which had never attracted my attention before: although they would often stop in the open, yet I shortly found that, photographically, they were not where they would make a negative. After several days, it dawned upon me that they always stopped in the shadow. Giving special attention to this point, I very soon found, on watching the deer which started up, that when they stopped for that moment of curiosity, as so often happens, it was almost invariably in the long shadows thrown by some trees across the park, or else in some shady part of the wood, and seldom by any chance where the sunlight shone directly upon them. This, while a matter of indifference to the hunter, is fatal to photographic success in this brilliant rarefied air, as it is almost impossible to get the details of any objects in the shadow without very much over-developing the high lights.

During the past season I found the elk very much wilder. They seemed to haunt the heavy timber, and to go to their wallows early in the morning or late in the evening, being scarcely ever seen in the open. I believe I should have succeeded much better had I waited till a month later, when the heavy snows would have driven them out of the higher country, as at that time they move in the daytime, and feed more in the open where the sun has bared the ground.

The game-photographer should always develop his own negatives, since the whole development is devoted to bringing out the details of the animals, regardless of the surrounding picture; and as these are so small, and blend so remarkably with the surrounding objects, the ordinary photographer is almost sure to overlook them.

In conclusion, let him who would get negatives rather than heads, possess his soul in patience, and carry all his energy and perseverance with him. If he is successful, his reward is ample from a sportsman's standpoint; if not, he will find a satisfaction in the chase not to be obtained by killing only.

W. B. Devereux.

Literature of American Big-Game Hunting

Throughout the pioneer stages of American history, big-game hunting was not merely a pleasure, but a business, and often a very important and in fact vital business. At different times many of the men who rose to great distinction in our after history took part in it as such: men like Andrew Jackson and Sam Houston, for instance. Moreover, aside from these pioneers who afterward won distinction purely as statesmen or soldiers, there were other members of the class of professional hunters—men who never became eminent in the complex life of the old civilized regions, who always remained hunters, and gloried in the title—who, nevertheless, through and because of their life in the wilderness, rose to national fame and left their mark on our history. The three most famous instances of this class are Daniel Boone, David Crockett, and Kit Carson: men who were renowned in every quarter of the Union for their skill as game-hunters, Indian-fighters, and wilderness explorers, and whose deeds are still stock themes in the floating legendary lore of the border. They stand for all time as types of the pioneer settlers who won our land: the bridge-builders, the road-makers, the forest-fellers, the explorers, the land-tillers, the mighty men of their hands, who laid the foundations of this great commonwealth.

Moreover, the class of men who follow hunting not as a business, but as the most exhilarating and health-giving of all pastimes, has always existed in this country from the very foundation of the republic. Washington was himself fond of the rifle and shot-gun, and a skilled backwoodsman; and he was also, when at his Mount Vernon home, devoted to the chase of the gray fox with horse, horn, and hound. From that time to this the sport-loving planters of the South have relished hunting deer, bear, fox, and wildcat with their packs of old-fashioned hounds; while many of the bolder spirits in the new West have always been fond of getting time for a hunt on the great plains or in the Rockies. In the Northeastern States there was formerly much less heed paid to, or love felt for, the wilder kind of sports; but the feeling in their favor has grown steadily, and indeed has never been extinct. Even in this part of the country, many men of note have been, like Webster, devotees of the fishing-rod, the shot-gun, or the rifle; and of late years there has been a constantly increasing number of those who have gone back to the old traditions of the American stock on this continent, and have taken delight in the wild sports of the wilderness.

Yet there have been fewer books written by Americans about life in the American wilderness and the chase of American big game than one would suppose,—or at least fewer books which are worth reading and preserving; for there does not exist a more dismal species of literature than the ordinary cheap sporting volume. This paucity of good books is, however, not unnatural. In a new country, where material needs are very pressing, the men who do the things are apt to be more numerous than those who can write well about them when done. This is as it should be. It is a good thing to write books, but it is a better thing still to do the deeds which are worth being written about. We ought to have both classes, and highest of all comes he who belongs to both; but if we had to choose between them, we would of course choose the doer rather than the writer.

Nevertheless the writer's position is very important; and there is no delusion more hopeless than the belief of many excellent people to the effect that the man who has done most is necessarily he who can write best. The best books are those written by the rare men who, having actually done the things, are also capable of writing well about them when done. It is as true of hunting-books as of those relating to graver matters, that in very many cases he whose experiences are best worth recording is himself wholly unable to record them. No amount of experience and observation can supply the lack of the literary gift. Many of the old hunters tried their hands at making books, but hardly a volume they produced is worth preserving, save possibly as material which some better writer may handle at a future time. Boone wrote, or rather allowed a small pedant to write for him, a little pamphlet on his early wanderings in Kentucky; but its only value is derived from the fact that for certain of the events in early Kentucky history it is the sole contemporaneous authority. The biography published by or for Davy Crockett is somewhat better, but it is hard to say what parts of it are authentic and what not. Of course a comparatively uneducated man may by some rare chance possess the true literary capacity; and the worst of all writers is the half-educated man, especially he who takes the newspapers as models whereon to found his style; while the mere pedant who takes his language solely from books and the school-room is but slightly better. But, taken as a rule, it may be stated that the man who writes well about life in the wilderness must not only have had long and thorough acquaintance with that life, but must also have had some good literary training.

There have been a few excellent books written by Americans upon the wilderness life and the wilderness game of this continent. Elliott's "South Carolina Field Sports" is a very interesting and entirely trustworthy record of the sporting side of existence on the old Southern plantations, and not only commemorates how the planters hunted bear, deer, fox, and wildcat in the cane-brakes, but also gives a unique description of harpooning the devil-fish in the warm Southern waters. General Marcy wrote several volumes upon life on the plains before the civil war, and in them devoted one or two chapters to different kinds of plains game. The best book upon the plains country, however, is Colonel Richard Irving Dodge's "Hunting Grounds of the Great West," which deals with the chase of most kinds of plains game proper.

Judge Caton, in his "Antelope and Deer of America," gave a full account of not only the habits and appearance, but the methods of chase and life histories of the prongbuck, and of all the different kinds of deer found in the United States. Dr. Allen, in his superb memoir on the bisons of America, and Hornaday, in his book upon the extermination of that species, have rendered similar service for the vast herds of shaggy-maned wild cattle which have vanished with such singular and melancholy rapidity during the lifetime of the present generation. Mr. Van Dyke's "Still-Hunter" is a noteworthy book which, for the first time, approaches the still-hunter and his favorite game, the deer, from what may be called the standpoint of the scientific sportsman. It is one of the few hunting-books which should really be studied by the beginner because of what he can learn therefrom in reference to the hunter's craft. The Century Co.'s magnificent volume "Sport with Gun and Rod" contains accounts of the chase of most of the kinds of American big game, although there are two or three notable omissions, such as the elk, the grizzly bear, and the white goat. Lieutenant Schwatka, in his "Nimrod in the North," has chapters on hunting the polar bear, the musk-ox, and the arctic reindeer.

All the above hunting-books should be in the library of every American lover of the chase. Aside from these volumes, which deal specifically with big-game hunting, there are others touching on kindred subjects connected with wild life and adventure in the wilderness which should also be mentioned. Of course all the records of the early explorers are of special and peculiar interest. Chief among the books of this sort are the volumes containing the records of the explorations of Lewis and Clarke; the best edition being that prepared by the ornithologist Coues, who has himself had much experience of life in the wilder regions of the West. Catlin's books have a special merit of their own. The faunal natural histories, from the days of Audubon and Bachman to those of Hart Merriam, must likewise be included; and, in addition, no lover of nature would willingly be without the works of those masters of American literature who have written concerning their wanderings in the wilderness, as Parkman did in his "Oregon Trail," and Irving in his "Tour on the Prairies"; while the volumes of Burroughs and Thoreau have of course a unique literary value for every man who cares for outdoor life in the woods and fields and among the mountains.

Our Forest Reservations

Few of the large animals of North America could exist save in a timbered country where shelter and hiding-places may be had. The wild creatures which live on the plains at once fall back before advancing settlements, and eventually, like the buffalo and the antelope, disappear; while the forest-inhabiting moose, deer, and elk, though in diminished numbers, still cling to their old-time retreats. The preservation of forests and of game go hand in hand. He who works for either works for both.

The preservation of our large game now has interest for a comparatively small class—the naturalist, the sportsman, and the lover of nature; while the preservation of forests, because of its direct bearing on the material prosperity of the country, is demanding more and more attention, and receiving a constantly growing appreciation. Intelligent action has been taken by National and State authorities in forest maintenance; public territories have been set aside as permanent possessions for the people. Since each new forest reservation means a new game refuge, a record of what has been done for public forests is a record of what has been done for game protection; and the review is one which affords abundant cause for satisfaction to all who are interested in the perpetuation of the large game of the continent.

A bill passed by Congress, March 3, 1891, contained a provision authorizing the President of the United States to set apart and reserve from time to time government lands wholly or in part covered with timber or undergrowth, as public reservations, and to declare by public proclamation the establishment of such reservations and their limits.

The passage of this law, while an essential step toward forest preservation, would have availed little unless acted on. Fortunately, General John W. Noble, who was Secretary of the Interior when the measure became a law, took a broad view of the importance of forest preservation. Early in his term of office he had recognized the great economic value of the Yellowstone Park as a source of water supply, and had given much attention to the protection of this reservation. The Yosemite Park also owes a great deal to his fostering care, and it was through him that the Grant and Sequoia Parks were set aside. When the enabling act of 1891 presented the opportunity, General Noble at once recommended the establishment of a number of forest reservations, and from time to time they have been set aside by presidential proclamation. Most of them include rough timbered mountain lands, unfit for cultivation or for settlement. They will serve by far their most useful purpose as timber reservations, natural reservoirs which will yield year after year a never-failing supply of water. Mr. Noble had the wisdom and the independence to lead public opinion rather than to follow it, and he set an example which it is hoped his successors will emulate.

Nor was he content to stop here. Realizing the rapidity with which commercial greed was sweeping out of existence important marine species of the Northwest, he caused Afognak Island, in Alaska, to be set aside as a perpetual reservation for salmon and sea-lions, and planned the establishment on Amak Island of a reservation for walrus, sea-otter, and sea-lions, and of still another on the Farallones for sea-lions and sea-fowl. These two refuges for the great marine mammals of our western seas have not yet been established, but the good work set on foot by Mr. Noble should be continued to completion with as little delay as possible.

Much more remains to be done. We now have these forest reservations, refuges where the timber and its wild denizens should be safe from destruction. What are we going to do with them? The mere formal declaration that they have been set aside will contribute but little toward this safety. It will prevent the settlement of the regions, but will not of itself preserve either the timber or the game on them. The various national parks are watched and patrolled by Federal troops, but even for them no provisions of law exist by which those who violate the regulations laid down for their care may be punished. The forest reservations are absolutely unprotected. Although set aside by presidential proclamation, they are without government and without guards. Timber-thieves may still strip the mountain-sides of the growing trees, and poachers may still kill the game without fear of punishment.

This should not be so. If it was worth while to establish these reservations, it is worth while to protect them. A general law providing for the adequate guarding of all such national possessions should be enacted by Congress, and wherever it may be necessary such Federal laws should be supplemented by laws of the States in which the reservations lie. The timber and the game ought to be made the absolute property of the government, and it should be constituted a punishable offense to appropriate such property within the limits of the reservation. The game and the timber on a reservation should be regarded as government property, just as are the mules and the cordwood at an army post. If it is a crime to take the latter, it should be a crime to plunder a forest reservation.

The national parks and forest reservations which already are, or by proper protection may become, great game preserves are those given in the list below. In these reservations is to be found to-day every species of large game known to the United States, and the proper protection of the reservations means the perpetuating in full supply of all these indigenous mammals. If this care is provided no species of American large game need ever become absolutely extinct; and intelligent effort for game protection may well be directed toward securing through national legislation the policing of forest preserves by timber and game wardens.

NATIONAL PARKS.

Yellowstone, in Wyoming, Montana, and Idaho.

Yosemite, in California.

Grant, in California, included in Sierra Forest Reserve.

Sequoia, in California, included in Sierra Forest Reserve.

FOREST RESERVATIONS,

Created under Section 24 of the Act of Congress of March 3, 1891 (26 Stat., 1095)—showing the locality of the reservations and the dates of the President's proclamations creating the same. Complete to March 20, 1893.

ALASKA.

Afognak Forest and Fish-Culture Reserve. Afognak Island and its adjacent bays and rocks and territorial waters, including among others the Sea Lion and Sea Otter Islands. Reserved under Sections 14 and 24, Act of March 3, 1891. Proclamation issued December 24, 1892.

ARIZONA.

Grand Cañon Forest Reserve. In Coconino County. Estimated area, 2893 square miles; 1,851,520 acres. Proclamation issued February 20, 1893.

CALIFORNIA.

San Gabriel Timber-Land Reserve. In Los Angeles and San Bernardino counties. Estimated area, 868 square miles; 555,520 acres. Proclamation issued December 20, 1892.

Sierra Forest Reserve. In Mono, Mariposa, Fresno, Tulare, Inyo, and Kern counties. Estimated area, 6400 square miles; 4,096,000 acres. Proclamation issued February 14, 1893.

San Bernardino Forest Reserve. In San Bernardino County. Estimated area, 1152 square miles; 737,280 acres. Proclamation issued February 25, 1893.

Trabuco Cañon Reserve. In Orange County. Estimated area, 78 square miles; 49,920 acres. Proclamation issued February 25, 1893.

COLORADO.

White River Plateau Timber-Land Reserve. In Routt, Rio Blanco, Garfield, and Eagle counties. Estimated area, 1672 square miles; 1,198,080 acres. Proclamation issued October 16, 1891.

Pike's Peak Timber-Land Reserve. In El Paso County. Estimated area, 288 square miles; 184,320 acres. Proclamation issued February 11, 1892; supplemental proclamation, March 18, 1892.

Plum Creek Timber-Land Reserve. In Douglas County. Estimated area, 280 square miles; 179,200 acres. Proclamation issued June 23, 1892.

The South Platte Forest Reserve. In Park, Jefferson, Summit, and Chaffee counties. Estimated area, 1068 square miles; 683,520 acres. Proclamation issued December 9, 1892.

Battlement Mesa Forest Reserve. In Garfield, Mesa, Pitkin, Delta, and Gunnison counties. Estimated area, 1341 square miles; 858,240 acres. Proclamation issued December 24, 1892.

NEW MEXICO.

The Pecos River Forest Reserve. In Santa Fé, San Miguel, Rio Arriba, and Taos counties. Estimated area, 486 square miles; 311,040 acres. Proclamation issued January 11, 1892.

OREGON.

Bull Timber-Land Reserve. In Multnomah, Wasco, and Clackamas counties. Estimated area, 222 square miles; 142,080 acres. Proclamation issued June 17, 1892.

WASHINGTON.

The Pacific Forest Reserve. In Pierce, Kittitas, Lewis, and Yakima counties. Estimated area, 1512 square miles; 967,680 acres. Proclamation issued February 20, 1893.

WYOMING.

Yellowstone National Park Timber-Land Reserve. On the south and east of the Yellowstone National Park. Estimated area, 1936 square miles; 1,239,040 acres. Proclamation issued March 30, 1891; supplemental proclamation, September 10, 1891.

NOTE. The areas given are the estimated aggregate areas lying within the exterior boundaries of the reservations. The lands actually reserved are only the vacant, unappropriated public lands within said boundaries.

The Exhibit at the World's Fair

At its last annual meeting the Club determined to have an exhibit at Chicago. It was felt that it would be a pity if at the World's Fair there was no representation of so typical and peculiar a phase of American national development as life on the frontier. Accordingly it was determined to erect a regular frontier hunter's cabin, and to fit it out exactly as such cabins are now fitted out in the wilder portions of the great plains and among the Rockies, wherever the old-time hunters still exist, or wherever their immediate successors, the ranchmen and pioneer settlers, have taken their places.

The managers of the World's Fair very kindly gave the Club for its exhibit the wooded island in the middle lagoon. Here the club erected a long, low cabin of unhewn logs; in other words, a log house of the kind in which the first hunters and frontier settlers dwelt on the frontier, whether this frontier was in the backwoods of the East in the days when Daniel Boone wandered and hunted in Kentucky, or later when Davy Crockett ranked not only as the best rifle-shot in all Tennessee, but also as a Whig congressman of note; or whether, as in the times of Kit Carson, the frontier had been pushed westward to the great plains, while new settlements were springing up on the Pacific coast and among the Rockies. The inside fittings of the cabin were just such as those with which we are all familiar in the ranch-houses and cabins of the wilderness and of the cattle country. There was a rough table and settles, with bunks in one corner, and a big open stone fireplace. Pegs and deer antlers were driven into the wall to support shaps, buckskin shirts, broad hats, stock-saddles, and the like. Rifles stood in the corners, or were supported by pegs above the fireplace. Nothing was to be seen save what would be found in such a cabin in the wilds; and, as a matter of fact, the various rifles, stock-saddles, and indeed the shaps and buckskin shirts, too, had all seen active service. Elk- and bear-hides were scattered over the floor or tacked to the walls. The bleached skull and antlers of an elk were nailed over the door outside; the head of a buffalo hung from the mid partition, fronting the entrance, inside; and the horns of other game, such as mountain sheep and deer, were scattered about. Without the door stood a white-capped prairie-schooner, a veteran of long service in cow-camps and on hunting expeditions.

The exhibit was put in charge of Elwood Hofer, of the Yellowstone National Park. On June 15 it was formally opened with a club dinner, at which a number of the gentlemen connected with the World's Fair were present as guests.

Big-game hunters visiting the Fair must have been especially struck with the colossal figures of moose, elk, bison, bear, and cougar which guard the various bridges; some are by Proctor, and some by Kemys. Well worthy of notice likewise were the groups of mounted big game in the Government Building, and those put up by Mr. L. L. Dyche in the Kansas State Building.

Constitution of the Boone and Crockett Club
FOUNDED DECEMBER, 1887.

Article I.

This Club shall be known as the Boone and Crockett Club.

Article II.

The objects of the Club shall be—

1. To promote manly sport with the rifle.

2. To promote travel and exploration in the wild and unknown, or but partially known, portions of the country.

3. To work for the preservation of the large game of this country, and, so far as possible, to further legislation for that purpose, and to assist in enforcing the existing laws.

4. To promote inquiry into, and to record observations on the habits and natural history of, the various wild animals.

5. To bring about among the members the interchange of opinions and ideas on hunting, travel, and exploration; on the various kinds of hunting-rifles; on the haunts of game animals, etc.

Article III.

No one shall be eligible for membership who shall not have killed with the rifle in fair chase, by still-hunting or otherwise, at least one individual of one of the various kinds of American large game.

Article IV.

Under the head of American large game are included the following animals: Bear, buffalo (bison), mountain sheep, caribou, cougar, musk-ox, white goat, elk (wapiti), wolf (not coyote), pronghorn antelope, moose, and deer.

Article V.

The term "fair chase" shall not be held to include killing bear, wolf, or cougar in traps, nor "fire-hunting," nor "crusting" moose, elk, or deer in deep snow, nor killing game from a boat while it is swimming in the water.

Article VI.

This Club shall consist of not more than one hundred regular members, and of such associate and honorary members as may be elected.

Article VII.

The Committee on Admissions shall consist of the President and Secretary and the Chairman of the Executive Committee. In voting for regular members, six blackballs shall exclude. In voting for associate and honorary members, ten blackballs shall exclude. Candidates for regular membership who are at the same time associate members, shall be voted upon before any other.

Article VIII.

The Club shall hold one fixed meeting a year, to be held the second Wednesday in January, and to be called the annual meeting.

Article IX.

This Constitution shall not be changed, save by a four-fifths vote of the members present.

List of Members
President.

Hon. Theodore Roosevelt,
Washington, D. C.

Secretary and Treasurer.

Archibald Rogers,
Hyde Park, N. Y.

Executive Committee.

W. A. Wadsworth,
Geneseo, N. Y.

George Bird Grinnell,
New York.

Winthrop Chanler,
New York.

Owen Wister,
Philadelphia.

Charles Deering,
Chicago.

Regular Members.

Hon. Benj. H. Bristow,
New York.

Col. James H. Jones,
New York.

Col. W. T. Pickett,
Meeteetse, Wy.

Col. H. C. McDowell,
Lexington, Ky.

Col. Roger D. Williams,
Lexington, Ky.

Hon. Henry Cabot Lodge,
Senate Chamber, Washington.

Hon. Bellamy Storer,
House of Representatives, Washington.

Albert Bierstadt,
New York.

D. G. Elliott,
New York.

Arnold Hague,
Washington.

Clarence King,
New York.

Thomas Paton,
New York.

John J. Pierrepont,
Brooklyn.

W. Hallett Phillips,
Washington.

E. P. Rogers,
Hyde Park, N. Y.

J. Coleman Drayton,
New York.

Elliott Roosevelt,
Abingdon, Va.

J. West Roosevelt,
New York.

Philip Schuyler,
New York.

Rutherfurd Stuyvesant,
New York.

Robert Munro Ferguson,
New York.

Royal Carroll,
New York.

William Milne Grinnell,
New York.

H. C. de Rham,
New York.

William B. Bristow,
New York.

H. N. Munn,
New York.

Percy Pyne, Jr.,
New York.

Frank Thomson,
Philadelphia.

J. A. Chanler,
New York.

W. A. Chanler,
New York.

R. D. Winthrop,
New York.

Hon. Boies Penrose,
Philadelphia.

C. B. Penrose,
Philadelphia.

R. A. F. Penrose, Jr.,
Philadelphia.

D. M. Barringer,
Philadelphia.

Frank Furness,
Philadelphia.

J. Chester Morris, Jr.,
Chestnut Hill, Pa.

B. C. Tilghman,
Philadelphia.

A. A. Brown,
Philadelphia.

John Sterett Gittings,
Baltimore.

James S. Norton,
Chicago.

W. J. Boardman,
Cleveland, O.

W. B. Devereux,
Glenwood Springs, Col.

Howard Melville Hanna,
Cleveland, O.

Dr. J. C. Merrill,
U. S. A., War Dept., Washington.

Charles E. Whitehead,
New York.

Lyman Nichols,
Boston.

Frank C. Crocker,
Portland, Me.

George H. Gould,
Santa Barbara, Cal.

Gen. A. W. Greely,
Signal Office, Washington.

Bronson Rumsey,
Buffalo, N. Y.

Lawrence Rumsey,
Buffalo, N. Y.

Dundass Lippincott,
Philadelphia.

Charles F. Sprague,
Boston.

Samuel D. Warren,
Boston.

Casper W. Whitney,
New York.

Douglass Robinson, Jr.,
New York.

Dean Sage,
Albany.

A. P. Gordon-Cumming,
Washington.

Henry L. Stimson,
New York.

Elihu Root,
New York.

James Sibley Watson,
Rochester, N. Y.

H. A. Carey,*
Newport, R. I.

James T. Gardiner,
Albany, N. Y.

Charles P. Curtis,
Boston.

Gen. W. D. Whipple,
Norristown, Pa.

Associate Members.

T. S. Van Dyke,
San Diego, Cal.

Col. Richard Irving Dodge,
New Rochelle, N. Y.

Hon. Wade Hampton,
Columbia, S. C.

Hon. Carl Schurz,
New York.

Gen. W. H. Jackson,
Nashville, Tenn.

Col. John Mason Brown,*
Louisville, Ky.

Major Campbell Brown,
Spring Hill, Tenn.

Hon. T. Beal,*
Washington.

Hon. G. G. Vest,
Senate Chamber, Washington.

Hon. Redfield Proctor,
Senate Chamber, Washington.

Dr. C. Hart Merriam,
Washington.

John Ellis Roosevelt,
New York.

W. Woodville Rockhill,
Washington.

Prof. John Bache MacMasters,
Philadelphia.

Edward North Buxton,
London, England.

Capt. George S. Anderson,
Yellowstone National Park, Wy.

Capt. Frank Edwards,
War Dept., Washington.

Capt. John Pitcher,
War Dept., Washington.

Major Moses Harris,
War Dept., Washington.

H. D. Burnham,
Chicago.

W. A. Buchanan,
Chicago.

Hon. Thomas B. Reed,
House of Representatives, Washington.

Honorary Members.

Gen. W. T. Sherman,*
New York.

Gen. Phil Sheridan,*
Washington.

Judge John Dean Caton,
Ottawa, Ill.

Francis Parkman,
Boston.

* Deceased.

www.ingramcontent.com/pod-product-compliance
Lightning Source LLC
Chambersburg PA
CBHW072155200426
43209CB00052B/1260